Jewels of the Wise
Self-Mastery Through the Tarot

Holy Order of MANS

Holy Order of MANS
Corte Madera, California

Copyright © 2012 Holy Order of MANS All Rights Reserved
Published by Holy Order of MANS, Corte Madera, CA
holyorderofmans.org

No parts of this book may be reproduced in any form or by any electronic or mechanical means, including information retrieval systems, without prior written permission from the author.

Cover and interior layout and design by Carolyn Oakley,
Luminous Moon Design + Press, Boulder, Colorado
luminousmoon.com

First Edition
First Printing: October 2022

ISBN-13: 978-1-7370176-8-4

Body, Mind & Spirit: Mysticism — Body, Mind & Spirit: Astrology — Body, Mind & Spirit: Alchemy

Printed and bound in the United States of America

Other Publications by Holy Order of MANS

The Golden Force
Keystone of the Tarot with Meditations
Tarot 22 Keys – The Major Arcana (tarot card set)
Stars of Heaven: Mystical Astrology

Forthcoming

Tree of Life

DEDICATION

Enter herein and see your perfect life unfold before your very eyes. Watch the symbols and signs closely as the Star within you takes you on a journey you'll never forget, again!

Jewels of the Wise: Self-Mastery Through the Tarot

Acknowledgments

Jewels of the Wise: Self-Mastery Through the Tarot was originally published by the Holy Order of MANS in 1967. By the late 1980's the Holy Order of MANS came apart and, consequently, their books were no longer available. Special thanks to Mark and Mary Anderson of the Science of Man who created a website in the 1990's and made these Order books available online. Special thanks to those who continued to do the Work of the Order during this time; and to Mary Ray who took on the daunting task of retyping most of the Order literature, including this book, in the mid 1990's, and putting it on the website www.HolyOrderOfMANS.org. Special thanks to Margot Whitney, Director, Holy Order of MANS who, in 2012, resurrected the Holy Order of MANS for the 21st century. Thank you to Cynthia Dietch Johnson for creating the line art of the cards, to Yimi Tong for her beautiful coloring of the cards, and to Carolyn Oakley at Luminous Moon Design for her patience and talented work designing and laying out the book and cover. And thank you to Michael Maciel, Director, Holy Order of MANS for his contributions toward the publication of this book.

Most importantly, and with heartfelt gratitude, we've placed our trust in God.

"…and Jesus looking upon them saith, 'With men it is impossible, but not with God; for with God all things are possible.' " (Mark 10:27)

Jewels of the Wise: Self-Mastery Through the Tarot

Introduction

One gem from many facets blazes fire,
One Light paints sacred scenes of stained-glass hue;
To just One Truth do many faiths aspire —
There is One Way, but many paths thereto.

Tarot represents the Path of Initiation and depicts the workings of mind and soul on the Way of Enlightenment. The purpose of *Jewels of the Wise: Self-Mastery Through the Tarot* is not to present novelty but to further serve the cause of Truth. All essentials basic to the teachings are retained, with such changes as have been revealed and given due consideration.

This book is not slanted for literary appeal but to bring together the simple fundamentals of universal Wisdom as depicted by the ancient symbols of Tarot, and to present them as clearly and constructively as possible. You must realize that, although study can lead you closer to attainment by opening up awareness, it is only after you have found some degree of Reality within yourself that the symbols can be really understood and appreciated.

We have not been told everything about each Key, because no one can. You have to find much of it yourself, and it cannot all become clear the first time around. But this material should provide an accurate and fruitful beginning to encourage the dawning Sun of Reality.

This work is taken from the ancient Cabala of the Hebrew teachings and is not fortune telling Tarot. We have not gone into divination. Why should anyone sit back and let circumstances tell him what to do, to have his "fortune" told for him, when he is supposed to tell it what to do? He is expected by degrees to learn self-mastery, as he is able. No matter what the divination tells you, it does not have to happen, unless you accept it and will permit it.

It is suggested you meditate on each Key for five or ten minutes as you read the chapters. And if you decide to color the cards, take them in exact chronological order, forgetting your own preferences, to encourage the correct process chosen by the Masters to unfold the Wisdom of their teaching.

For until you have studied one Key, or opened one door, you are not ready for any of those which follow. It is also recommended that after reading the entire book (not too fast), you could gain further by rereading the first three chapters, and pondering the ancient quotations.

Coloring instructions, symbology in a nutshell, and meditations are given in the companion book *Keystone of The Tarot with Meditations*. Available for coloring your personal Tarot cards is a black and white deck *Tarot 22 Keys – The Major Arcana*. Additional understanding of the planets and their symbolism in the Tarot may be found in *Stars of Heaven: Mystical Astrology*.

In studying the cards individually, you can generally consider the background as representing that which has come before, or the past, and the foreground as that which depicts the present or future condition.

Let us assure you that the studies presented here are in no way derogatory to the teachings of any religious faith, but are designed to amplify spiritual understanding in all of them.

The Holy Order of MANS is an organization dedicated to a more thorough understanding of the universal laws of the Creator so that all might better manifest God's Creation and thus promote Peace and Harmony among people everywhere. Our purpose is to teach the Ancient Christian wisdom to this new generation as it was taught in the past.

Our organization is called the Holy Order of MANS because the universal laws of creation, the law of prayer, and other principles can be taught and, in your everyday life, you can become the master of your fate through conscious application of these principles.

We use the term "man" to include both men and women.

Jewels of the Wise: Self-Mastery Through the Tarot

Contents

Dedication v

Acknowledgments vii

Introduction ix

Holy Order of MANS xi

The Cabala and the Tree of Life 15

The Twenty-Two Letters 25

The Origins of Tarot 31

The Cube of Space 35

The Four Suits 37

Tarot Tableau 41

Tarot – Correspondences Chart 44

The Twenty-Two Keys (0-21) 47

<u>Illustrations</u>

Tree of Life 14

32 Paths of Wisdom on the Tree of Life (chart) 24

William Blake 1794 30

Cube of Space 35

Tarot Classic Deck 36

The Tarot Tableau 40

Tarot – Correspondences Chart 1 44

Tarot – Correspondences Chart 2 45

Jewels of the Wise: Self-Mastery Through the Tarot

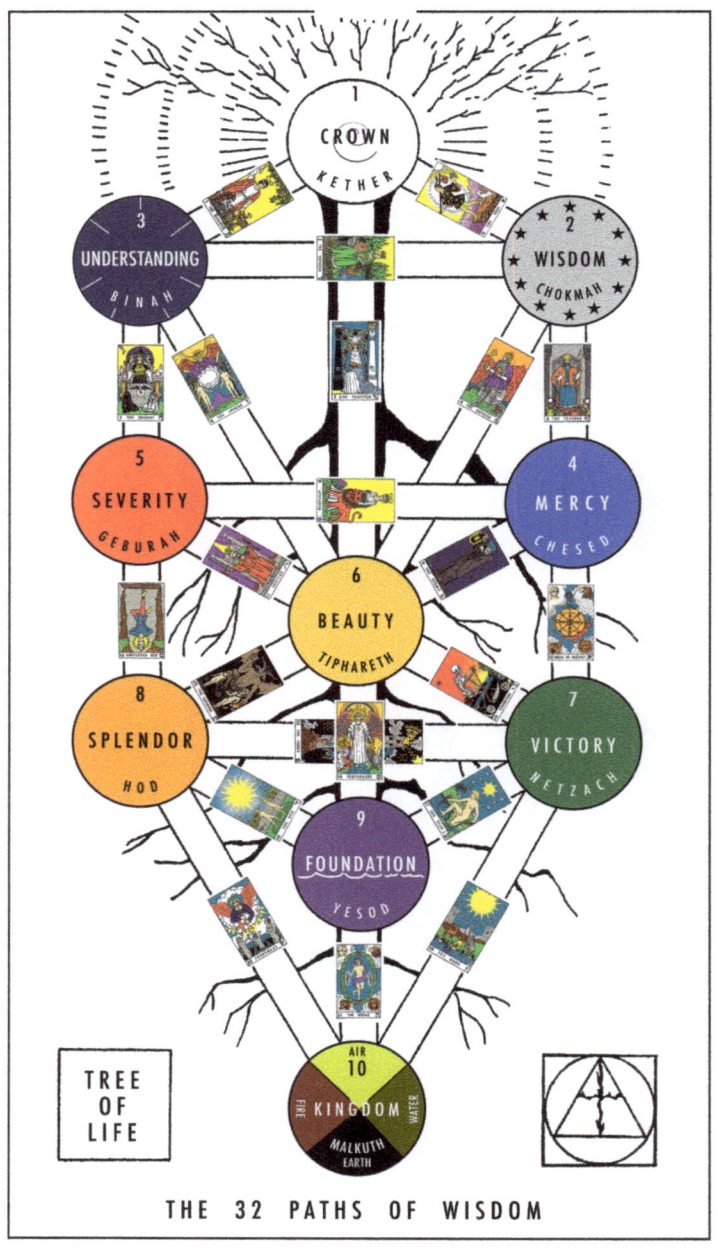

The Cabala and the Tree of Life

Cabalism has been called the great poem of Judaism—"a Tree of Symbolic Jewels showing forth the doctrine of the Universe as the vesture of Deity."

The Cabala also provides an enlightening background to the teachings of Tarot, although the two subjects can be studied quite independently, and each found complete in itself. Their common link rests in the Tree of Life and its 32 Paths, based on the mystical significance of the same twenty-two letters attributed to the Major Arcana Keys of Tarot.

The Tree of Life is the creative Power manifesting through the various facets necessary for it to manifest, as God spoke the Word of Creation into His universe. The Tree is depicted, one might say, like a map of Creation showing the channels or Paths leading from God to His creation and back again, and through which the ancients attempted a minute study of each part in order to arrive at the whole.

It is shown upside-down, because spiritual or Eternal Life can only be rooted in that which is above us in consciousness, not in the sky, of course, but in the inner, finer provinces of the heaven worlds, where senses geared to grosser physical life cannot reach. In this context, "above" and "within" are identical in meaning. Nor is this inner realm related to the physical body directly.

The only physical manifestation of the Tree of Life is its fruit, a very small part of which can be seen by earthly eyes in the world of the four elements. This is the product or end result of the Tree. In this the Tree of Life is unlike any growth begun from the material standpoint, where roots are temporarily anchored in the perishable earth below our feet.

The Tree of Life is described in the Bible in both the first and last books. In the beginning, the man of earth and his mate were driven from the vicinity of the Tree, before having tasted of its wondrous fruit; but in the last chapter of Revelation the Tree of Life reappears in the New Jerusalem to be enjoyed by spiritually-realized humanity. Two trees, in fact, were there, to provide the "happy ending" after a long and arduous journey.

Cabala, also spelled Qabalah, or Kabbala, is a Hebrew word which means "a thing received," and refers to the reception and transmission of divine revelation of the secret or hidden tradition and unwritten divine Law. Unlike the traditions of the Pharisees, which were based on custom and regulations, these teachings are not the literal or historical version of the Law as understood by the majority, but are comprised of those meanings which were passed along only to initiates, and usually by word of mouth. Some like to think this teaching began back as far as Abraham, or even Adam.

The Ten Spheres on the Tree of Life diagram shown are called Sephiroth, a Hebrew word meaning "Emanations" or "Numberings" (the many from the One). Some Rabbis believed the word "Sapphire" was also derived from Sephirah, because the Ten Spheres were called the Shining Sapphires which reflected the Light from the center of Kether, the Crown.

Beginning from the top, these Sephiroth, or Spheres, are called a "progressive materialization of Ideas in the Mind of God." Each is shown as a separate state in manifestation—a stage of God's Emergence, and all show phases of Creative Evolution. Then on the Way of Return when man lifts his consciousness to a higher level, a series of increasingly abstract refinements are experienced through the mystical initiations, as he draws nearer to the Fount or Source of all.

The Universe is described as having come about by the issuing of pure spiritual Substance from God; thus, the elements that were later to make up the universe were always potential in the Godhead.

The first known written work on the Cabala was the *Book of Formation,* traditionally supposed to have originated nearly two thousand years ago, but in proven circulation since the fourteenth century. Let us quote portions of this poetic work:

> "Yah, the Lord of Hosts, the living Elohim, King of the Universe, Omnipotent, Dweller in the Height whose habitation is Eternity…engraved His Name, and ordained and created His Universe in thirty-two mysterious Paths of Wisdom, by means of the three forms of expression, namely: Numbers, Letters, and Sounds, which are in Him one and the same."

> "Ten Sephiroth (ten properties from the Ineffable One), and twenty-two letters are the Foundation of all things. Of these twenty-two letters, three are called Mother letters, seven double letters, and twelve simple letters."

> "The ten numbers out of Nothing are analogous to the ten fingers and ten toes: five over against five. In the center between them is the covenant with the Only One God. In the spiritual world, it is the covenant of the voice (the Word), and in the corporeal world the circumcision of the flesh."

> "Ten are the numbers out of Nothing—ten, not nine; ten, not eleven. Comprehend this great Wisdom, understand this knowledge and be wise. Inquire into the mystery and ponder it. Examine all things by means of the ten Sephiroth. Restore the Word to Its Creator and lead the Creator back to His throne again. He is the only Formator and beside Him, there is no other. His attributes are ten, and are without limit."

"The ten ineffable Sephiroth have ten infinitudes, which are: The infinite Beginning and the infinite End; the infinite Good and the infinite Evil; the infinite Height and the infinite Depth; the infinite East and the infinite West; the infinite North and the infinite South; and over them is the Lord Superlatively One, who rules over them for ages of ages."

"The appearance of the ten spheres out of Nothing is as a flash of lightning or a sparkling flame, and they are without beginning or end. The Word of God is in them when they go forth and when they return. At His bidding do they haste like a whirlwind and prostrate themselves before His throne."

"The ten Sephiroth have their end linked to their beginning, and their beginning linked to their end, conjoined as the flame is wedded to the live coal; for the Lord is Superlatively One and to Him there is no second. Before One, what can you count?"

"Concerning the number of the spheres of existence (the Sephiroth) out of Nothing, seal up your lips and guard your heart as you consider them, and if your mouth opens for utterance and your heart turns toward thought, control them, returning to the silence. So it is written: 'And the living creatures ran and returned.' (Ezekiel 1:14) And on this wise was the covenant made with us."

"These are the ten emanations of Number out of Nothing."

They represent the successive Divine Emanations which constitute creative evolution, and are sometimes drawn like a flash of Lightning, zig-zagging from one to another in order of the numbers, the whole being shown hilted like a fiery Sword.

All ten are eternal, and they are the Substance of all that is—the form to be supplied by the twenty-two letters. They represent the contrast between substance and form, and creation must resolve that contrast with God as the solvent. In this Way, Existence, or the combination of form and substance, takes on reality.

The Ten Sephiroth are in essence described below. The Hebrew translation is in parenthesis. See the Tree of Life diagram on page 14.

Numerically, the Zero does not represent one of the Spheres, but rather the background of the whole Tree, and the Absolute, or Nameless Root of all manifestation. It suggests the Radiant darkness out of which emerges the first Light, while its circular form symbolizes totality and eternity, and non-being in the sense of being without qualification. It is the Cosmic Egg from which all Creation and all numbers emerge.

Sphere 1. CROWN *(Kether)* is the name of the first Sphere. It symbolizes the mystical point and irradiating center, or First Force of Whirling Energy, at the nucleus of the circle and the Egg. Here occurs the focusing of Power and the initiating of all things.

Sphere 2. WISDOM *(Chokmah)* is called the second power of God. It is located at the top of the right Pillar on the Tree, and represents the Father Principle in Creation; the fiery Life Force which is the generating principle of all the numbers, and the beginning of polarity.

Sphere 3. UNDERSTANDING or INTELLIGENCE *(Binah)*, the third power of God, third point on the Supernal Triangle, and the Mother Principle in all Nature, situated at top of the left Pillar of the Tree. As the Life Force starts to limit itself, there begins a condensation of energy for the substantiation of form, and the beginning of generation. From her comes forth the seven lower spheres.

Sphere 4. MERCY or GREATNESS *(Chesed)*, the fourth power of God, represents Cosmic Memory looking back to the Source of all, and demonstrating Beneficence, mildness, and might. The first day of Biblical creation.

Sphere 5. SEVERITY or STRENGTH *(Geburah)*, the fifth power of God. Immutable operation of Cosmic Law, whose workings seem severe to those not acting in accord therewith. The Dynamic Law of Sphere 5 proceeds from the Abstract Order of Sphere 4, producing the balance of Mercy with Justice.

Sphere 6. BEAUTY *(Tiphareth)*, the sixth power of God. Cosmic Son-Sun, and Divine Love. Harmony, symmetry, and balancing of all opposites. Center of the Tree, and Mediator between archetypal worlds above, and human realms below.

Sphere 7. VICTORY *(Netzach)*, seventh power of God. Mastery through Victory over the desire nature. Realm of Venus and emotions. The fourth day of Biblical creation.

Sphere 8. SPLENDOR or GLORY *(Hod)*, eighth power of God, and of the Intellect. Balances with Victory opposite. Vibration and infinity. Hermetic teachings; realm of Mercury.

Sphere 9. FOUNDATION *(Yesod)*, the ninth power of God, Omnipotent. The astral and lunar realm of the formative state of consciousness, the automatic consciousness, and the heaven world.

Sphere 10. KINGDOM *(Malkuth)*, is the tenth power of God. Outward manifestation of creation, the kingdom of heaven established in the world of the four elements. The number 10 indicates completion of a cycle or orb, ready to start over on a higher level, always moving in spiral fashion, and evolving upward.

There are but ten fundamental questions in the universe. Each corresponds to an attribute.

In treading the thirty-two Paths on the Tree of Life, you first receive fully from each what can be absorbed as you go. Then, having finished the journey, and arrived at the place where fruit manifests in Light and Wisdom, you begin to give forth to others of that which has been received, and to rise higher in consciousness on the Way of Return over the same Paths from a different perspective, where you are the driver rather than the passenger.

These paths are not really separate, but act as thirty-two different aspects of awareness of One Single Reality, much as a jewel flashes light from one facet or another, each being but different expressions of One Whole.

"In thirty-two mysterious Paths of Wisdom did God write. He created His Universe by the three forms of expression: Numbers, Letters, and Words." It is a combination of these which is called the Speech of God. "How did He fuse them together—stones as letters, houses as words?"

The Ten Spheres of Emanation make up the first Ten Paths of Thirty-Two. They represent the Macrocosm and are based upon Number. To each of these spheres is given a name as well as a Number.

COLORING THE TEN SPHERES ON THE TREE OF LIFE

PATH ONE   Crown *(Kether)*: White

PATH TWO   Wisdom *(Chokmah)*: Gray

PATH THREE   Understanding *(Binah)*: Indigo

PATH FOUR   Mercy *(Chesed)*: Blue

PATH FIVE   Severity *(Geburah)*: Red

PATH SIX   Beauty *(Tiphareth)*: Golden-yellow

PATH SEVEN   Victory *(Netzach)*: Green

PATH EIGHT   Splendor *(Hod)*: Orange

PATH NINE   Foundation *(Yesod)*: Purple

PATH TEN   Kingdom *(Malkuth)*
- Air, at top: Citron (green plus orange)
- Fire, at left: Russet (orange plus violet)
- Water, at right: Olive (violet plus green)
- Earth, at bottom: Black

Paths eleven through thirty-two refer to the twenty-two Major Arcana Tarot Keys, and are colored as noted in the coloring instructions for each Key.

"In Thirty-Two wonderful Paths of Wisdom did Jah decree and create His universe, by means of three kinds of characters: Numbers, Letters and Words. To the Ten spheres of Emanation, He assigned Numbers, and these refer to the Macrocosm. To the channels between these Spheres, He assigned twenty-two Letters, which refer to the relationship between Macrocosm and Microcosm."

The Cabala and the Tree of Life

32 Paths of Wisdom On the Tree of Life

Path		Color	Symbol	Sphere
1	Crown	white	◎	1
2	Wisdom	gray	⁎⁎⁎	2
3	Understanding	blue-violet	♄	3
4	Mercy	blue	♃	4
5	Severity	red	♂	5
6	Beauty	yellow	☉	6
7	Victory	green	♀	7
8	Splendor	orange	☿	8
9	Foundation	purple	☽	9
10	Kingdom (Four Elements)	earth colors	⊗	10

Path		Color	Key	Hebrew Letter	Letter
11	Fool	yellow	0	א	A
12	Magician	yellow	1	ב	B
13	High Priestess	blue	2	ג	G
14	Empress	green	3	ד	D
15	Emperor	red	4	ה	E
16	Teacher	red-orange	5	ו	V
17	Lovers	orange	6	ז	Z
18	Chariot	orange-yellow	7	ח	Ch
19	Strength	yellow	8	ט	T
20	Hermit	yellow-green	9	י	Y
21	Wheel of Fortune	violet	10	כ	K
22	Justice	green	11	ל	L
23	Suspended Man	blue	12	מ	M
24	Transition	blue-green	13	נ	N
25	Temperance	blue	14	ס	S
26	Deceiver	blue-violet	15	ע	O
27	Tower	red	16	פ	P
28	Star	violet	17	צ	Ts
29	Moon	violet-red	18	ק	Q
30	Sun	orange	19	ר	R
31	Judgement	red	20	ש	Sh
32	World	blue-violet	21	ת	Th

The Twenty-Two Letters

Between the Ten Spheres of Emanation run twenty-two Channels or Paths to each of which is assigned a sound—twenty-two sounds for the twenty-two letters of the Hebrew alphabet. The Paths represent the relation between Macrocosm and Microcosm, and also, the Grades or Stages of Initiation. As steps of Soul-unfoldment, or phases of subjective development, they lead one on toward conscious realization of the Cosmos. They are sometimes called Ways, or degrees of Manifestation of the Divine Life-Force.

Of the letters, it is said: they are designed and appointed by God, for "God drew them, hewed them, combined them, weighed them, interchanged them, and through them produced the whole Creation and everything that is destined to be created." He established them, formed by the breath, and by breath impressed them upon the air.

God spoke the Word of Creation. The Word is made up of sounds, and sounds are identified by symbols called letters. The twenty-two letters depict all possible words.

It is said that these twenty-two letters by their various combinations are the means by which the laws of the universe are established, and constitute the "scepter of the Almighty which He wields from his flaming throne in the Higher Realm. He created a reality out of Nothing. He called the non-entity into existence and hewed colossal pillars from intangible air."

Jewels of the Wise: Self-Mastery Through the Tarot

Through understanding of the letters, we reach to the Name or Source, which is the object of contemplation. Jesus, Himself, was called the Word made flesh, and our own spiritual development comes about as a result of the Word.

Let us quote further from the ancient *Book of Formation*, sometimes called the "Ladder of Truth":

> "When the Patriarch Abraham had comprehended the Great Truths and meditated upon them, the Lord of the Universe appeared to him, called him "Friend," kissed him on the head and made with him a covenant. He bound the spirit of the twenty-two letters upon his tongue, and disclosed to him their secrets. God permitted the letters to be immersed in water, He burned them in the fire, and imprinted them upon the winds."

There are twenty-two basic sounds and letters. Three are the first elements, fundamentals, or Mothers—Fire, Air, and Water, (Shin, Aleph, and Mem). Seven are the double letters, and twelve are the simple letters.

THE MOTHER LETTERS

The three Mother Letters are: Sh, A, and M, the basic elements from which all manifested creation originates. Assigned to them are the attributes realization, superconsciousness, and reversal.

Key 20	Sh	Shin	Fire	Realization
Key 0	A	Aleph	Air	Superconsciousness
Key 12	M	Mem	Water	Reversal

THE SEVEN DOUBLE LETTERS

The seven double letters—B, G, D, K, P, R, and Th—are so designated because to each is assigned the Intelligence or attribute of a pair of opposites. Each has a duplicity of pronunciation as two voices, and can be spoke aspirated or unaspirated. They also signify the dualities to which mankind is exposed—the hardness and softness, the weakness and strength. For while these seven symbolize the gifts of wisdom, riches, fertility, life, power, peace and grace, they also signify their opposites. Assigned to them are the seven planets.

Key 1	B	Beth	Life & Death	Mercury
Key 2	G	Gimel	Peace & Strife	Moon
Key 3	D	Daleth	Wisdom & Folly	Venus
Key 10	K	Kaph	Wealth & Poverty	Jupiter
Key 16	P	Peh	Grace & Sin	Mars
Key 19	R	Resh	Fertility & Sterility	Sun
Key 21	Th	Tav	Dominion & Slavery	Saturn

THE TWELVE SIMPLE LETTERS

The twelve simple letters are attributed to the signs of the zodiac, and to each is assigned a definite function. Those representing the five senses and speech are mentioned first, thus:

Key 4	E	Heh	Aries	Sight
Key 5	V	Vav	Taurus	Hearing
Key 6	Z	Zain	Gemini	Smell
Key 7	Ch	Cheth	Cancer	Speech
Key 8	T	Teth	Leo	Taste (Digestion)
Key 9	Y	Yod	Virgo	Touch
Key 11	L	Lamed	Libra	Action
Key 13	N	Nun	Scorpio	Motion
Key 14	S	Samekh	Sagittarius	Wrath
Key 15	O	Ayin	Capricorn	Mirth
Key 17	Ts	Tzaddi	Aquarius	Meditation
Key 18	Q	Qoph	Pisces	Sleep

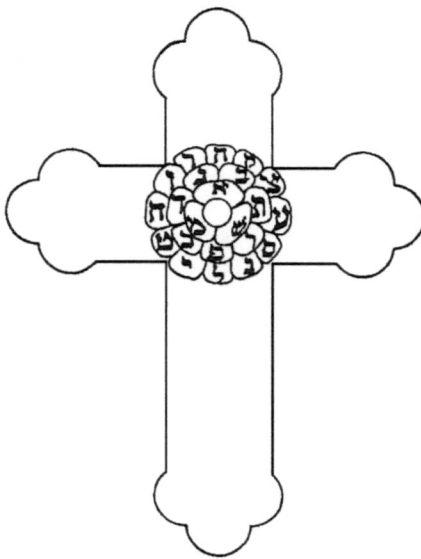

The Rose of Unfoldment

Sometimes the Rose Cross is shown with a flower of twenty-two petals. The outer circle petals correspond to the twelve simple letters. The second row of seven petals corresponds to the seven double letters. The three Mother letters make up the inner row.

The Twenty-Two Letters

The Ancient of Days in Europe a Prophecy copy B from the Glasgow University Library
William Blake, Public domain, via Wikimedia Commons

The Origins of Tarot

The Tarot is a book of pictures in symbolism common to all sacred teachings since the most ancient times. Each picture depicts a different version of the great universal Truths.

These symbols were designed with great care by spiritual Masters of Wisdom that they might awaken within each who perused them a recognition of his true Self.

We think more vividly in pictures than we do in words, so that a picture impressed on our minds is easier to remember than the same lesson not illustrated. These pictures are called Tarot Keys, and the symbols do act as Keys to unlock, one by one, the secret chambers of our soul's memories of that Divine Source from whence we came. In that sense, they are not something that must be learned, but rather they help to uncover through association that which we already know.

These pictures become painted in Light upon our inner consciousness, and each admits one portion of the whole Light, just as stained-glass windows of a great cathedral tell of various events, but the Light they diffuse is all from the same Source.

The origins of Tarot are hidden in the archives of time; for no one knows definitely when and where to place the beginning of this ancient book of pictures. In a day when spiritual knowledge was highly suspected, and books were being burned which did not agree with the current religious or political ruling, what better way to hide the sacred Wisdom Teachings than to put them out in plain sight, among a set of "foolish" pictures? They could be carried in anyone's pocket, and hidden under the crude cover of a game in case they were found.

These symbols are so simply used that only the initiate would notice them. The Fool himself is a clue to their secret. Sufi masters often played the part of fools to put across their teachings in action rather than words. And the royal court jester of old was often a very wise man who by calculated antics was subtly able to advise a king.

The Sufis claim that Tarot forms an allegory of the teachings of a Sufi master about certain cosmic influences upon humanity, and that the word "Tarot" derives from the Arabic *turuq* meaning "four ways," in view of the division of the pictures into four elements of four "suits" when brought down into playing cards. The word *tariquat* means "the way" reminiscent of the TAO, the Way of Lao-tse. Another source says the word comes from the Sanskrit, and means "fixed star," symbolizing immutable tradition.

Others say it derives from *Tarosh*, from the *Book of Thoth*, of Egyptian origin, and that it signifies the symbolical presentation of universal ideas. Symbols on the cards include motifs common to the Rosicrucians, the Masons, the Qabalists, the Egyptians, Pythagoras, and the old alchemists.

One tradition is that a group of adepts from all over the world gathered in Morocco to pool their great Wisdom in pictorial symbols that would transcend the language barrier. Again, we are told that the Knights Templar brought these cards back secretly from the Crusades, having taken them from the Saracens, and used them for amusement and gambling. Whether they were concealed to hide the fact of their theft, is not known.

At about the same time Gypsies began to wander around Europe, and they used cards for telling fortunes. Gypsies were first officially mentioned in English books of law about the time of Henry VIII, where they were described as an outlandish people, "calling themselves Egyptians, who do not profess any craft or trade, but go about in great numbers."

The Origins of Tarot

A legend indicates that after the destruction of the Serapeum in Alexandria, the large number of attendant priests banded together seeking means to preserve secrets of the rites of Serapis. Their descendants carried with them the most precious of the volumes saved from the burning library—the Book of Enoch, or Thoth (Tarosh). These later became wanderers upon the earth, remaining a people apart with an ancient language and a birthright of magic and mystery. This great library, by the way, burned for a whole week, wiping from memory much of man's recorded learning.

It is said in some of the ancient Egyptian initiations the initiate was led through a long gallery in which were hung life-sized pictures of all the Tarot Keys, and he was required to spend enough time before each picture to achieve some sort of realization of the significance of that Key. A legend still more ancient states that the Tarot teachings were brought out from ancient Atlantis. Obviously, these teachings were not limited to any single culture, and their story, if it could be fully traced, would be most fascinating.

Jewels of the Wise: Self-Mastery Through the Tarot

THE CUBE OF SPACE

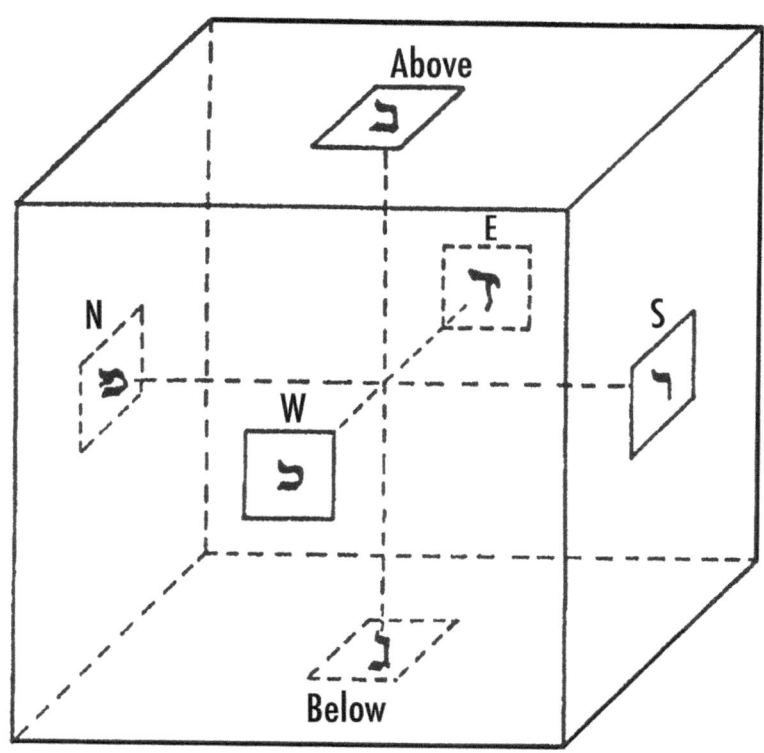

Tav is placed at the centermost point of the Cube of Space, the Place of the Presence, or the Shekinah. The seven double or planetary letters form the six faces and central point of the Cube, while the twelve simple letters represent the twelve boundary lines. Three remaining letters cross the Cube and represent the Elements Air, Fire, and Water. That place which stands in the center of all is called the Holy Habitation of God.

From Jean Dodal's *The Tarot of Marseilles* (Wikipedia.com, public domain)

The Four Suits

In the mystery teachings, we are concerned almost entirely with the twenty-two trumps, or Major Arcana, in which the symbols are "hidden." The word "trump" was derived from "triumph," because they were triumphant over the lesser cards, while "arcana" refers to an inner secret or mystery.

The Minor Arcana, the numbers one through ten of each of the four "suits," are seldom studied. There is little to say of their meaning except that they are concerned with the activities of the ten Sephiroth in each of the four elements, whereas the twenty-two major Keys act as connecting links, Paths or Channels, between the Sephiroth on the Tree of Life.

The entire deck consists of seventy-eight cards—our regular playing deck of fifty-two plus the twenty-two trumps—and the addition of four Pages or messengers (boys or girls), as well as the Kings, the Queens, and the Knights (Jacks) who are usually shown as horsemen, quite understandably, as the Spanish and French words for "knight," *caballero* and *chevalier*, mean "horseman."

Clubs — Wands

The cards which we call clubs (or, in French *trefoils*, trifoliate, for the three-part leaves) are in Tarot drawn as sticks or clubs, and called wands. These represent the element of Fire or light, Will and the

Spirit. Creatively, they represent the realm of abstract ideas, nearest the top of the Tree of Life.

Hearts — Cups

Our so-called hearts are shown as cups and represent the element of water; the state of fluidity; and the creative World, or plane, the fluidity of plastic Mind-Stuff which, through creative thinking, is stirred by the abstract ideas of the Spiritual Plane.

Spades — Swords

The suit of spades is pictured as swords. This derives from the Spanish word *espada* which means "sword" and represents the element of air or gases. This is the plane of activity which puts plans into motion and draws together the materials needed.

Diamonds — Coins or Pentacles

The fourth suit is that of the earth element, or solidity. These, the diamonds, were formerly shown as coins or pentacles. This suit represents the final result or outcome in the world of Material manifestation of the four elements, and of the mineral kingdom, as shown at the bottom of the Tree of Life.

The four "court cards" are symbolic of: the King, Spirit; the Queen, Soul; the Knight, personal energies; and the Page, body. (Again, the four planes of creation.) Each is modified by the suit it represents, as is also each of the numbers one through ten which correspond to the ten Spheres, or Sephiroth.

The Four Suits

Jewels of the Wise: Self-Mastery Through the Tarot

Tarot Tableau

The accompanying Tarot tableau of cards is arranged with both columns and letters of the alphabet reading from right to left. The Hebrew language is always written in this way, and this arrangement permits The Fool to move forward into the manifestation of all of his potential.

Many new facets will appear as you study the relationships between Keys in this formation. The Fool, himself representing the element Air, moves toward Gemini and Libra, both Air signs. The Ox is touched by the Ox-goad; and the sword of Justice meets the Sword (Zain, Key 6).

Vertical row one deals with Thought and the function of mentality, moving down toward the speaking of the Word. Row two is concerned with various functions of the alchemical Water. Row three is devoted to growth and change, primarily in the area of the subconscious. Row four deals with different degrees of accomplishment. Row five shows a series of triplicities.

We expect that your own study or meditation will open new vistas and possibilities. One of the best means of understanding the individual Keys is to study them in relation to others.

According to an old belief, the Hebrew alphabet was derived from groups of stars, with fixed stars for consonants, and the luminaries or planets for vowels. In this starry handwriting, words were written on the walls of the heavens, which, if one could read them, spelled out the meanings of all things.

And if we turn back to about four or five thousand years ago in India, Shiva spoke to Devi thus: "Imagine the Sanskrit letters in these honey-filled foci of awareness, first as letters, then more subtly as sounds, then as most subtle feeling. Then, leaving them aside, be free."

Tarot Tableau

Jewels of the Wise: Self-Mastery Through the Tarot

Path No.	Title	Color	Hebrew Names & Letters	
1	Crown	White	Kether	Sephirah 1
2	Wisdom	Gray	Chokmah	Sephirah 2
3	Understanding	Blue-violet	Binah	Sephirah 3
4	Mercy	Blue	Chesed	Sephirah 4
5	Severity	Red	Geburah	Sephirah 5
6	Beauty	Yellow	Tiphareth	Sephirah 6
7	Victory	Green	Netzach	Sephirah 7
8	Splendor	Orange	Hod	Sephirah 8
9	Foundation	Purple	Yesod	Sephirah 9
10	Kingdom	Citron Russet X Olive Black	Malkuth	Sephirah 10
11	The Fool	Yellow	Aleph (A) Ox	Key 0
12	The Magician	Yellow	Beth (B) House	Key 1
13	High Priestess	Blue	Gimel (G) Camel	Key 2
14	The Empress	Green	Daleth (D) Door	Key 3
15	The Emperor	Red	Heh (silent H or E) Window	Key 4
16	The Teacher	Red-orange	Vav (U, V, W) Nail or Hook	Key 5
17	The Lovers	Orange	Zain (Z) Sword	Key 6
18	The Chariot	Orange-yellow	Cheth (Ch) Fenced Field	Key 7
19	Strength	Yellow	Teth (T) Snake	Key 8
20	The Hermit	Yellow-green	Yod (I, Y, J) Open Hand	Key 9
21	Wheel of Fortune	Violet	Kaph (K) Closed Hand	Key 10
22	Justice	Green	Lamed (L) Ox-goad	Key 11
23	Suspended Man	Blue	Mem (M) Seas	Key 12
24	Transition	Green-blue	Nun (N) Fish	Key 13
25	Temperance	Blue	Samekh (S) a Prop	Key 14
26	The Adversary	Blue-violet	Ayin (O) Eye	Key 15
27	The Tower	Red	Peh (P, Ph, F) Mouth	Key 16
28	The Star	Violet	Tzaddi (Tz, Ts, Cz) Fish-hook	Key 17
29	The Moon	Violet-red	Qoph (Q) Back of Head	Key 18
30	The Sun	Orange	Resh (R) Head or Face	Key 19
31	Judgement	Red	Shin (Sh) Tooth	Key 20
32	Cosmos	Blue-violet	Tav (T, Th) Mark	Key 21

Tarot Correspondences Chart

Astrological Correspondence	Function		Intelligence (Insight) of Path
Limitless Light	Primal Will	First Beginnings	The Admirable Intelligence
Firmament of Fixed Stars	Life Force	Creative Energy	The Illuminating Intelligence
Saturn	Divine Soul	Primordial Root or Matter	The Sanctifying Intelligence
Jupiter	Cosmic Memory	Preservation	The Receiving Intelligence
Mars	Cosmic Law	Volition	The Radical Intelligence
Sun	Christ Center	Mediation	Intelligence or Mediating Influence
Venus	Instinctive Forces	Feeling and Vitalizing	The Hidden Intelligence
Mercury	Thought Forms	Perfection through Intellect	Perfect or Absolute Intelligence
Moon	Vital Soul	Etheric or Astral	The Purified Intelligence
Earth	Physical Realm	Manifestation	The Resplendent Intelligence
Uranus	AIR Superconsciousness	Divine Life-Breath	The Fiery Intelligence
Mercury	Conscious Mind	Attention	Intelligence of Transparency
Moon	Subjective Mind	Reflection	The Uniting Intelligence
Venus	Creative Imagination	Growth	The Luminous Intelligence
Aries	Reason	Sight	The Constituting Intelligence
Taurus	Intuition	Inner Hearing	Triumphant & Eternal Intelligence
Gemini	Discernment	Smell	The Disposing Intelligence
Cancer	Receptivity – Will	Speech	Intelligence of House of Influence
Leo	Suggestion	Taste	Intelligence of Secret of Spiritual Activities
Virgo	Way-shower	Touch	The Intelligence of Will
Jupiter	Cosmic Cycles	Rotation	The Rewarding Intelligence
Libra	Action (or Deeds)	Equilibration	The Faithful Intelligence
Neptune	WATER – Silence	Reversal	The Stable Intelligence
Scorpio	Change	Transformation	The Imaginative Intelligence
Sagittarius	Vibration	Verification	The Intelligence of Probation
Capricorn	External Appearances	Mirth	The Renewing Intelligence
Mars	Destruction of Error	Awakening	The Exciting Intelligence
Aquarius	Meditation	Revelation	The Natural Intelligence
Pisces	Sleep	Organization	The Corporeal Intelligence
Sun	Directing Principle	Regeneration	The Collective Intelligence
Pluto & Vulcan	FIRE Breaking down Form	Realization	The Perpetual Intelligence
Saturn	EARTH Spiritual Attainment	Cosmic Consciousness	The Administrative Intelligence

The Twenty-Two Keys

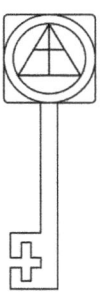

Path 11
The Fiery Intelligence

Superconsciousness *Planet Uranus*

Key 0

THE FOOL

Letter A   **Aleph – Ox**

> *"I am the Alpha and Omega, the beginning and the ending.."* (Revelation 1:8)

It has been said that the entire mystery of Tarot is wrapped up in the symbolism of the Zero card called the Fool, whose letter is A. The Hebrew word for this first letter of the alphabet is Aleph, translated "Ox."

Each of the twenty-two major trumps of Tarot is correlated with one of the twenty-two letters which comprise the Hebrew alphabet, these being taken in order all the way through.

Why the picture representing pure Spirit and the element Air should coincide with a letter which means Ox or Bull is at first difficult to ascertain; for astrologically, the Bull is a symbol for the solid-earth sign, Taurus.

Yet, in the sketch below representing the evolution of the letter A, note the similarity of the Taurus symbol to the Sinai letter A. The alphabet was designed during the Age of Taurus, which covered a period roughly between 2000 to 4000 B.C. This was an agricultural era when oxen were a source of motive power and strength, as well as being sacred to certain deities such as Apis and Jupiter. The Indian god Mithra is shown mounted on a bull.

So, it was natural that this symbol should stand at the head of the alphabet in honor of their gods.

Egyptian	Sinai	Phoenician	Greek	Roman
3000 B.C.	*1850 B.C.*	*1200 B.C.*	*600 B.C.*	*114 A.D.*

In the teachings of Tao and Zen, we find references to the mystical Bull which symbolizes the Eternal Principle of Life and Truth in action as well as Creative Energy and the taming of natural forces. The Ten Bulls of Zen represent a sequence of experiences concerning the realization of true Being, and the steps of awareness which lead to understanding of the Creative Principle.

Since the Zero Key becomes the first channel of force to move out from the Sphere of the Crown atop the Tree of Life, it is said to represent the Eternal Power which will continue to manifest in the remaining twenty-one Keys in a more limited form.

Because all the others exist in the abstract substance that is represented by Zero, it becomes their common denominator; for like the egg it resembles, Zero includes the full potential of all the others, but each must be experienced in order to unfold its reality.

In an older version of this Master Key, the Fool was depicted much larger and wearing the remaining twenty-one Keys spread out upon his garment in rows of 1, 2, 3, 4, 5, and 6.

Aleph stands above all and before all, poised, and ready to descend through all; for he represents the Absolute Unity of the All-pervading Presence of the Universe.

Before anything ever began, preceding all form or numeration, Nothing was there—just the Absolute or No Thing. Even a Zero, which is the first symbol of nothing, when it is drawn or named, becomes "something," like a bit of the Radiant Darkness enclosed and defined.

This Key relates to the element Air as the Divine Life-Breath of God. "Life-Breath" is the correct meaning of the Hebrew word *Ruach*, which is variously translated in the Bible as "the Soul," the

"Holy Ghost," and "Spirit." This is helpful to know in Bible study. Latin *Spiritus* also means both "Breath" and "Spirit," as does the Greek *Pneuma*. Sanskrit *Prana* has much the same connotation.

As the number Zero, this Key represents the inhalation of the Divine Breath *before* the beginning of Creation, as an expectant hush lay over all the formless void before God spoke the Creative Word. In that Breath are all things contained which are to come forth, though nothing as yet is manifest; for in Breath is contained Spirit and in Spirit is contained Life.

Jesus said in John 3: 8, "The wind blows where it will, and you hear the sound thereof, but cannot tell whence it comes, nor whither it goes; so is every one that is born of the Spirit."

Like the Cosmic Egg, Zero represents the One Reality which precedes all beginnings, and sums up all things within Itself, thus containing within Itself the full potential of growth and development prior to "hatching." It is No-Thing in that one can neither measure nor define it. It includes every imaginable possibility of that to come while yet free from any limitation of form or attribute.

Some ancient myths tell us that Creation came forth from a Cosmic Egg. "The Swan of the Empyrean has laid the egg of manifestation in the darkness of the Cosmic Night. "

The red feather worn by The Fool symbolizes that king of the air, or bird of the Spirit, the eagle in action. In Egyptian symbology, the Feather of Truth, Maat, was weighed in the balance scales opposite the heart when the soul's judgment had come.

The Fire of Spirit descending into matter demands Air first of all, even as a baby is not really alive until it catches its first breath. And while life may be sustained for some time without food (corresponding to the element Earth), or without water, it could last but minutes without Air. When breathing finally stops, the Spirit soon withdraws and the silver cord is severed which held body and soul together. The first form of radiant energy from the Sun which we learn to use is Air —controlled by breathing.

The yellow background relates both to the element Air and to the intellect—sometimes also to solar energies.

Uranus is the planet associated with this Key, and it relates to the unusual or the unexpected. Uranus tends to bring about sudden changes, especially when it comes to dissolving any outgrown or crystallized conditions which stand in the way of progress. *Ouranos* is a Greek word meaning "heaven," and Uranus was the grandfather of the gods and of the heaven realm.

Before a thing is manifest, one must accept its outcome on faith and take the plunge however "foolish" it may appear. Had Lot's wife not held back, she would not have crystallized. There is no place for hesitation when the True Spirit beckons. "For the wisdom of this world is foolishness with God." (1 Corinthians 3:19)

The word "Fool" comes from a Latin word *Follis* meaning both "bag of wind" and "bellows" (by which air is forced to stir up a fire). Paul was proud to be called a Fool for Christ, a wise fool, in obedience to the Light.

Here we are shown the symbol of Christ, the white spiritual Sun behind The Fool, showing from whence he came. He is as the Soul coming out from the Eternal which passes into the darkness of the physical body before returning again to the height.

This picture represents the inmost Self, standing on the brink of any new venture. But look not down, lest that become your destination. The goal is *up*, and there let your gaze be turned in order that every move you make, however it outwardly appears, becomes a step upward. The expected step into manifestation symbolizes the descent of spirit into matter in order to manifest in physical form or in some kind of action. The outcome will bring him to that still higher level on which his attention is fastened.

While he seems to have reached the end of his journey, we know that the attainment of any goal is but the arrival at a point of change, or new beginning of another enterprise. He represents Cause, the

The Fool: Key 0

I AM within you, which sees far beyond the seeming limitation of your present circumstances and brings the desire to improve.

The valley is the field of experience as well as the abyss or the "Mother-Deep" of Eastern terminology. There the phenomenon of Effect takes place.

The Life-Power he depicts is always at "the morning of its might," forever young, and forever poised at the brink of manifestation. The possibilities of this experience always transcend anything that has gone before.

He wears a white undergarment to show underlying purity while the white rose carried over from the past shows freedom from lower forms of desire and passion, along with cultivation of pure spiritual desire. This appears to have been plucked from the rosebush of Key 13 Transition.

He has come from high attainment represented by the snow-white peaks behind him, and still taller ones lie ahead.

The little white dog represents intellect at the personal level; the Egyptians used a dog as symbol of the Intellect. Our thinking mind acts as friend and companion while we keep it pure, quiet and well-trained. But it must be kept under control and ruled, remembering that your mind is far less important than the Self of God within you.

The Fool carries a wand which is the symbol of Will and of measurement. Its black suggests the command or use of occult (hidden) powers. The pouch suspended thereon is his bag of memories—the summed-up essence of all his past experiences being carried forward, and this is all one can bring from one incarnation to another. The All-Seeing Eye, in place of a lock, says that we must use spiritual Sight as a means of unlocking its secrets.

As he girds himself with the belt of Time to come into dense manifestation, the colorful cloak lined with the red force of passion and active energy will conceal the underlying purity (the white garment) during his sojourn. He cannot remove this garment until he again removes the belt representing limitations imposed by Time-

Consciousness and learns to live timelessly—to substitute Eternity for Time.

The eight-pointed star and the lunar crescent denote respectively the solar (electric) and lunar (magnetic) currents of energy—two modes of One Life Force.

The eight-spoked wheels on his garment depict solar orbs, or points of whirling creative Force prior to manifestation; for eight is a solar number. There are ten of them as there are Ten Spheres on the Tree of Life, plus one additional sphere of flame to depict activation of the heart center.

In another sphere is written the Hebrew letter Shin, symbol of the Holy Spirit. Around each are seven florets of green, the color and number of Venus, to suggest the activity of the Venus-ray in vegetation wherein Nature is bound, while the three-lobed leaves reflect both the ideas of Key 3 The Empress and the Trinity.

"Let no man deceive himself. If any man among you seemeth to be wise in this world, let him become a fool, that he may be wise." (1 Corinthians 3:18)

HE IS SPIRIT IN SEARCH OF EXPERIENCE.

The Fool: Key 0

Path 12
Intelligence of Transparency

Attention *Planet Mercury*

Key 1

THE MAGICIAN

Letter B **Beth – House**

Beth is the letter wherewith Creation began, and its number 1, the number of beginning.

In reference to Genesis, we see the first creation. "And God said, Let there be light; and there was light." (Genesis 1:3)

The Hebrew Bible began with the letter Beth, and in the same way, anything we want to initiate in our own lives must begin with the things this letter stands for.

That is because the Key called the Magician refers to pure Intellect, to the conscious mind and personality of an individual, and to the original activity and creative power of Man. Every action you perform must begin with thought, or mental awareness, and the energy to transfer that thought into action.

The Magician has also been called The Alchemist or The Minstrel in some versions, but his mission is the same. He represents the individual standing as a channel between that which resides above him, and that below.

At each step of these studies, we carry over the potencies of the preceding Key—in this case, bringing the Life-Breath of The Fool down from the heavenly realm to the sphere of human life. Briefly, Spirit descends into Matter where it proceeds to occupy or clothe itself with an outer vehicle—its house of mentality and personality while on earth.

Our thoughts are the real houses we live in. If we don't like them, we are at liberty to change or "move out" and make new ones at any moment. Your mind could be considered a homesteader staking his claim and if he dwells there long enough, that state of mind becomes legally his home.

Beth means "house," though a more ancient form of the letter depicted it as an arrowhead, because we aim our thoughts as arrows toward the goal of our endeavors. As a house, we act as habitation for the Divine Life-Breath.

One is told that "except the Lord build the house, he labors in vain that builds it." That which man attempts with personal or selfish willfulness carries with it no Life-Force, but is like man-made machinery which abides a little while, and then fades away. For by blocking the flow between God and the goal, man has cut off the Source of Life from his efforts.

The Magician in this lesson is too wise for this. He holds up a white wand, the emblem of purified will, depicted as a hollow tube through which the Power from Above is allowed to flow.

The uplifted wand is a symbol of the sublimation of vital forces through a giving-over of one's personal will to the Will of God. The resultant influx of Power from above enables him to transform and transmute that which is below, himself serving as a channel of the Force, like Mercury, a messenger rather than an originator.

Whereas The Fool stood at a superhuman level above and before all things, The Magician is the beginner and initiator of all things in human terms on the level of man's consciousness.

First, The Fool looked up to determine a true and ultimate goal which must be in accord with Infinite Cause in order to "work." (The aim of the Alchemist is perfected humanity.) Next, as he occupies a "house" of mind and personality, he must go to work, first relating to that Source of power which is above before he can start. As Jesus said, "Of myself, I do nothing; the Father which dwelleth within me, He doeth the works. "

The Magician: Key 1

It behooves us to take care what we think about. For negative thoughts and words provide the weeds for your own garden of life. This power of higher Mind goes to work on the automatic or subconscious realm where growth and development takes place, as in a garden—you know not how. You merely plant and water and cultivate. You watch and pray, and in time, the fruits appear.

The blooms here being cultivated show the active desire nature (roses) of human love and beauty, beside the pure-minded aspect (lilies), which are six-pointed, as the Star of David. These represent universal Love to which he is pointing attention. The roses number five because desire usually relates to one of the five senses while four lilies stand for the four primary aspects of Truth correlating with the four elements.

The arbor of roses overhead is a shelter achieved by the culmination of previous gardening endeavors. These have grown to such height as to hang overhead, giving him new incentive to keep active and continue work, as echoed also by the color red (action and energy) of his outer cloak. He will accomplish much as the result of his continual attention and prayer for right action! He has accomplished the work of the roses and is now directing more attention toward the unfoldment of lilies.

The Magician is related to Mercury as shown by the yellow color in the background. This color is also related to the element Air and the Intellect.

As the swift messenger of Mind, Mercury acts as a conveying element from one world into the other. He is also associated with Hermes, the Thrice-Great Teacher of occult mysteries and of the ancient Hermetic Wisdom. Quicksilver, or Mercury, is used in thermometers because it reacts instantly to heat expansion, and again is symbolized as a messenger between the above and below.

This is the Master Builder and the original Alchemist, working with all his tools laid out in order before him on the architects' workbench or Trestleboard. These tools represent the fundamental principles in Nature called "the four elements," that is: *Fire*, the Wand of Will and Energy; *Water*, the Cup of Knowing and Imagination; *Air*, the Sword of Daring and Craftsmanship; and *Earth*, the Coin of Silence and of Materialization. He uses these to deal with conditions in his life.

The number One fittingly designates this Key, for "1" represents all beginnings and here is the beginning of action and creation. "1" also shows a single, upright figure, simple and direct. Being vertical, it shows action. His eye is single, for only thus can results be free from scattering or confusion.

He is the Onlooker, the Director, and our everyday waking consciousness. As you actively plant and cultivate all day long (not just at prayer time), stop and note the nature and quality of your seeds, moment by moment, for a clue to life-conditions.

Because the mind can really think of just one thing at a time, a program of "positive thinking" would leave little room for negative thoughts.

His white inner robe shows underlying purity of intent and the Light of Truth which enables him to achieve desired results. The white headband binds back and controls dark locks of natural inertia and ignorance, which instinctively resist one's efforts to rise. The circle on his headband is of silver to suggest the lunar activity of the pineal gland, while the golden wings signify the uplifting power of solar energy.

Whereas The Fool girded himself with a belt of Time to descend into Matter, The Magician has bound himself with the girdle of Eternity, or Timelessness, and with occult attainment. His blue-green belt, the color of Scorpio, signifies sublimated serpent power.

Above his head is another symbol of the Infinite in the horizontal number 8. Both girdle and the number 8 are looking ahead to Key 8 (Strength) which shows the potential development of subconscious forces to equal those of the conscious mind.

The Magician: Key 1

The control and development depicted in all subsequent Keys can only come about as the direct result of taking this initial step. You have to start everything in mind. But when you are meditating, and feeling in tune with the Infinite, don't "jump back into the room" of your thoughts.

Path 13
The Uniting Intelligence

Memory *Planet Moon*

Key 2

THE HIGH PRIESTESS

Letter G   **Gimel – Camel**

She sits as Soul within the blue of the temple walls,
God's temple being Man.

"The world was without form, and void, and darkness was upon the face of the deep; and the 'Spirit,' 'wind,' or 'Breath' of God was moving over the face of the waters." (Genesis 1:2) All are one word, Ruach, and refer back to the Life-Breath of The Fool.

"And God said, Let there be a firmament in the midst of the waters, and let it divide the waters from the waters." (Genesis 1:6) The waters relate to the Cosmic mind-stuff, or the universal invisible substance out of which all was fashioned. The High Priestess represents the virginal subconscious, or pure Divine Substance.

She sits with passive authority just below the level of conscious awareness. Though these aspects of her being are not always interchangeable, she represents at different times and ways, the Soul, the subconscious mind, the Akasha, and the Cosmic Mind-stuff. She is called the Mother-Root and primary principle of Matter in its virginal state.

From her gown flows the substance of Cosmic Mind-Stuff in rippling streams like water throughout the universe, and this is the source of every stream you see pictured throughout the Tarot series. The stream will terminate in Key 20, Judgment, where the substance has become at this higher level "fixed," congealed into "icebergs."

The color blue is used to symbolize this esoteric "water" which begins as a river of Light. Though invisible, having weight, it is called the "gravitational force of the Radiant Energy" of the universe.

She represents all virgin goddesses—Diana of the Moon in particular, Isis, and Eve before her marriage. She wears the silver crown of Isis composed of the waxing, waning, and full moons. As "Queen of the borrowed Light," the moon reflects the idea of alternation and cyclic phases. The crown also suggests the horns of a bull, and the moon's exaltation in Taurus. The diamond is a symbol of light and brilliance, or the Mystical Center. Here it is used to denote the spiritual force streaming through the pineal gland to activate the sight center.

This Key is called the purest and most exalted concept of the Moon. Its crescent cup shows receptivity and its meanings clearly picture lunar attributes, even to the number two. Two is most apt for this Key relating to rhythm, cycle, and repetition. It also suggests duality, duplication, reflection, memory, and polarity, or "twoness"—just as the mirror reflects the "one" back to itself, seeming "two."

The polarities—light and dark, positive and negative, good and evil, hot and cold, and all other opposites—are but two extremes of one idea.

Photography works with these extremes, bringing out a true printed likeness through the use of light and dark contrasts. Without contrast, there would be no picture. If all the black and white in the play of light and shadow were blended and united into gray, there would be no visible outlines. Yet, gray is the symbol of wisdom where shown in the Tarot, because the Wise Man no longer looks upon good-and-evil, but sees all as One.

The cameraman of the series is The Magician of Key 1. He, Conscious Mind, snaps mental pictures continuously throughout his waking hours. These pictures are impressed upon the medium represented by The High Priestess and in turn developed by The Empress, Key 3—all within yourself.

She does not choose what pictures The Magician will snap; therefore, negative, careless thoughts or worries take pictures as well as those carefully posed.

The alertness of our observations determines the clarity of the recorded experience. "There is nothing hid which shall not be manifested; neither was anything kept secret but that it should come abroad."

As a sidelight observation on the negative side of the feminine nature, an unwise person tends to unreel experiences at high speed in minute detail as though every thought and experience, however trivial, had to be told, whether the other person wanted to hear it or not, as though her function were that of an automatic recorder with compulsion to playback.

On the higher side, this function of Memory is necessary to the orderly working of the laws of nature, as they express in perfect sequence the Life Power from above.

This thread of consciousness which runs through the chain of our lives and links them together may be compared to a microfilm record of all our experiences, and their summation the condensed essence which our soul carries through lives. Gimel is also called the link between the archetypal and formative worlds.

All that has ever previously happened is held in her lap in the form of a scroll representing the Akasha (the Akashic Records) or Cosmic Memory. The Hindus sometimes equate the Akasha with sound, a primordial or Universal Sound out of which creation and the elements emerged.

On the scroll is printed the word Tora, a Hebrew word meaning "Law," and representing immutable Cosmic Law. Her right hand is hidden to show that the more powerful activities of subconsciousness elude ordinary perception; for while The Magician works outwardly, she works from beneath her cloak.

Her seat of stone symbolizes union with the Father while its square shape is that of the cube, one of the symbols of earth. Because salt crystallizes into cubes, the term "salt" in alchemy refers to the element of earth, or of manifestation on the material plane. Salt is also symbolic of the "mystical sea of the Virgin," the great sea of Cosmic Substance.

Her throne rests upon the (yellow) foundation of mental activity, and is placed, one might say, in the Temple of Solomon, or on the Porch of Isis—both being symbolic of deeper truths. This picture draws somewhat on the Biblical symbolism of King Solomon's Temple.

"He set up the pillars at the vestibule of the Temple; he set up the pillar in the south and called its name Jachin, and he set up the pillar on the north, and called its name Boaz. And upon the tops of the pillars was lily work: so was the work of the pillars finished." (1 Kings 7:21-22)

The lily work referred to in the Bible is shown here as a lotus bud at the top of each pillar to indicate the undeveloped potential of the subconscious mind.

We see the initials of these two names, Yod and Beth, on the two pillars. The name *Jachin* means "He will establish," whereas the name Boaz means "in a strength. "

The initial B, or Beth, on the dark, negative pole stands for the strength which stems from resistance, the inertia or negation which resists our efforts. Beth represents the beginning of an endeavor, which is rooted in darkness, as a plant rooted in soil. At top of this pillar rests a bowl of water, akin to the astral element active in formation, and to the receptive or passive expression of Divine Energy.

Atop the positive or white pillar stands a bowl of flame, according to ancient temple practice, and this symbolizes Spirit and the active expression of Divine Energy. Its initial Yod is called the Life-Principle and Divine Will. This pillar stands for the progress of a matter in Light, or the positive establishing principle of all things.

The white pillar is situated on the South side, or the side of Light, while the dark pillar is on the North, the side untouched by the Sun;

hence, considered the darkness of the Unknown. Together, the message of the two implies: "In Strength shall My House be Established."

The Priestess seated between these two opposite poles acts as an agent of equilibrium, or mediator between light and darkness, and between initiative and resistance. The cross at exact center of the Key indicates the uniting of these opposites; thus, is this Path called The Uniting Intelligence.

A tree grows sturdier for the wind which hurls against it, being forced to draw on inward strength in order to resist, whereas overprotection would tend to foster weakness.

The same principle applies to using something against which to brace one's feet when making a great effort to lift a weight, or to climb. The block which one uses as a footstool provides a solid basis from which to reach higher and do better work. Abraham Lincoln once said he was grateful for his father's opposition to his efforts for an education because it gave him "something to brace his feet against."

The greater the temptation by which one is surrounded, the greater is the strength that can be developed by one who is able to resist. Man needs the external with which to evolve his soul until he has learned to evolve within himself.

Pomegranates were used on priestly vestments in Biblical times. One of their meanings is the reconciliation of multiplicity (the many seeds) within unity (the shell). Here the red pomegranates show feminine fruitfulness as the green palms suggest the masculine polarity, but their colors are reversed—the red normally being a color of masculine Mars and the green of feminine Venus. This reversal of color symbols is suggestive of the astral plane ruled by the moon and of a film negative where color is reversed. This helps to bring about the transposition into the gray of the veil—a color of Wisdom and the union of all opposites thus blending.

The Biblical pillars were set up at the entrance to the vestibule leading into the nave before the inner sanctuary. The veil behind the throne is the symbol of virginity, here referring to the virginal subconscious mind, or stream of human consciousness. The white veil upon her head suggests both purity and AUR, or Light—the "third veil of the Absolute."

The Hebrew letter *Gimel*, G, shown with this Key means "camel." The idea relates to travel and commerce as a thread or link between desert towns and settlements where the camel was once man's only link with the outside world, carrying news, goods, and learning. The obedient camel carried his own water supply with him—like unto the stream of consciousness. With the beginning or setting up of any practice, repeated performance of an art or ritual, thought or pattern, forms a thread of continuance which carries it forward into firmly established fact (or form).

As the camel squeezed through the "needle's eye," or a passage through the walls of Jerusalem, the consciousness must unload its pack of unnecessary memories, possessions, and habits to slip through the straight and narrow spiritual gate and to enter the Kingdom of Heaven—within oneself; for one cannot squeeze through a gate blocked by inward fatness, but must become as unleavened bread, free of earthly bubbles. The word in Aramaic is *gamla*, and means "camel," "a large rope" or "a beam." A large rope would likewise find it difficult to pass through a needle's eye.

"Thou art clothed with honor and majesty, Who coverest Thyself with Light as with a garment, Who hast stretched out the heavens like a tent, Who has laid the beams of Thy chambers upon the waters." (Psalm 104)

The High Priestess: Key 2

Path 14
The Luminous Intelligence

Imagination *Planet Venus*

Key 3

THE EMPRESS

Letter D **Daleth – Door**

"And a great portent appeared in heaven, a woman clothed with the sun, with the moon under her feet, and on her head a crown of twelve stars. She was with child." (Revelation 12:1)

The path of The Empress is called The Luminous Intelligence. She is the bright and shining one whose radiance stems from the solar light within, like the rays which cause the sun itself to be visible to our eyes.

She refers not to outer activity, which belongs in the realm of her masculine counterpart, Mars, but rather to the more subtle inner impulse, and to subjective experience. In other words, she represents Venus as the principle of growth, the eternal urge to love, the desire to unify and harmonize all conditions, and to attract and weld together those factors which complement each other.

As Empress (a word derived from "She who sets in order"), she deals with order on the inner level and correlates factors within the subconscious to harmonize and balance them.

The river flowing in the background stems from The High Priestess' gown, and shows the underlying stream of consciousness now in active operation—water flowing forcefully to produce a waterfall. A fish swims beneath the surface in token of the hidden life within subconsciousness.

Pearls are related both to the moon and to Venus; and their number, seven, a Venus number, also represents the seven chakras, here strung together in order at the throat area—again ruled by Venus.

The gold edging of neck and girdle indicate the solar forces which are an aid to her work.

The stone bench elaborates on the simple wisdom of the stone cube used by The High Priestess. Venus always elaborates on Nature, cultivating the natural so it becomes "artistic," and transforming the commonplace into the beautiful.

A function of this Key is Imagination, or embroidering fact with fancy to elaborate the outcome.

Looked upon as a woman "with child," The Empress is called the power from which emanates the entire tangible universe. But growth here is all on the inner, or hidden planes corresponding to the subconscious mind. As Mother Earth, she depicts the inner pulse of creation awaiting the call of spring to show forth new growth.

"And God said, Let the earth bring forth grass, the herb yielding seed, and the fruit tree yielding fruit after his kind, whose seed is in itself, upon the earth: and it was so." (Genesis 1:11)

The Virgin Mary is usually pictured wearing blue and white to represent virginal purity. But en route to Bethlehem, she could appropriately have worn a green cloak. A green robe is also traditionally worn by the Patriarch of Zen Buddhism. It is the color of nearly all vegetation which covers the Earth, and of chlorophyll leaf-coloring, which both draws sunlight to itself and emanates a substance back toward the sun in reciprocal action.

The main symbol in Key 3 is the heart. In the Tarot the right hand is the active hand. She's holding a seven-sided copper shield, as the metal assigned to Venus, which is also used for coins. Its seven sides refer again to Venus with its rulership of love; for the higher aspect of love is The Empress' real protection. Copper symbolizes the desire nature, which negatively based may act as the tempter, but when positive helps pull one toward redemption. The seventh Sphere on the Tree of Life, called Victory, is that of Venus.

This symbol on the shield is the descending dove. The dove represents the Holy Spirit, or Life Force. Here it's seen moving on the shield of love. Meaning is found in the heart. The heart is a symbol of the mystic spiritual center within man. It came to be associated with love due to the importance of love in the mystical teachings of unity, though the heart is actually related to the sun, rather than to Venus. It was said by the old philosophers that the heart takes precedence over the brain as the true seat of intelligence.

To connect to The Empress you must practice love. We can approach nature through science, but the direct approach is through the heart, through feelings.

A red triangle over her heart (emphasizing the number 3 of the card) shows the Law being activated, the outcome not yet manifest. The Greek letter *Delta* is drawn as a triangle, and corresponds to our letter D, or in Hebrew *Daleth*. Also the letter of this Key, *Daleth*, translates as "Door"—specifically the leaf of a door.

The door indicated here is the passageway between worlds, even as the womb is called the door to physical life. As the means of exit and entrance between inner and outer life, it swings either way. Love itself is a great door to the hearts of others.

♀ The symbol for Venus shows a circle above a cross, or spirituality taking precedence over matter. The four elements are symbolized by the cross. The Venus symbol is also used in biology and medicine to represent the feminine principle. The Empress is holding a scepter of authority shaped like an upside-down Venus, or literally a Mars symbol. Her authority, at this level, is based upon the potential of motherhood, as indicated by the position of the scepter.

The red masculine color of Mars used for the triangle and the roses of love and desire shows that an actual "detectable energy" is at work in the midst of all the underlying automatic growth.

The direction East denoted by this Key intimates the rising point of higher consciousness. This is the place of sunrise, and Venus is called the "bright and morning star," being the brightest of planets, the nearest to Earth, and so near the sun that it can only be seen at sunrise or sunset. Its orbit is just inside that of Earth. The Empress provides the Portal and Gateway of the Sun.

The fact that she is crowned with twelve stars represents the influence of the twelve signs of the zodiac through which celestial forces and modes of Cosmic Activity pour energy into her atmosphere. These twelve are shaped as six-pointed Stars of David ("Beloved") showing the workings of "above" to be like unto those "below."

The moon under her feet indicates accomplishment of those things; it represents the underlying powers of subconsciousness and her intellectual (yellow or Mercurial) understanding thereof. The yellow background also shows that behind her is the power of intellect which proceeds from the Magician.

Cypress tree were anciently sacred in worship of the goddess Venus, and the evergreen myrtle leaves woven into a wreath for her head were also a symbol of love. There are ten cypress trees, indicating the ten Sephiroth. A dove is in one of the trees, symbolizing Venus, peace and the Holy Spirit.

Wheat ears show the multiplication of seed in growth and increase, as well as her relation to Earth goddesses such as Ceres and Isis, which she also represents.

There is also a bee in the cypress trees. The bee in Egyptian hieroglyphics was related to royalty, because of the organization of the hive. It also signifies wealth and industry, while the sweetness of honey is suggestive of Venus. Bees were sometimes used in Christian symbolism to represent the virtues of Mary.

Whereas The Fool depicts a state just preceding manifestation at the Cosmic level, or Spirit itself about to enter matter, The Empress represents the Door and the process through which that Life must pass to enter the physical realm.

It has been said: "All intellectual light, like all physical light, comes from the East."

Path 15
The Constituting Intelligence

Reason *Sign Aries*

Key 4

THE EMPEROR

Letter E or silent H **Heh – Window**

I utter Myself by Seeing.

The Empress in the previous Key was shown exercising passive but loving control over growth and formation in the unseen realm. Things have to develop within before they show externally. But when anything manifests, or becomes outwardly visible, the conscious mind takes over the authority. Only after she has presented him with a child can he act in the capacity of a father, taking the responsibility of directing his progeny.

When something is projected from inside yourself to the outside, it is first seen by the eyes as though you peered out through a window. Thus is sight the function of this Key.

The letter *Heh* is the equivalent of E, or silent H. It means "window," which is a contraction of "wind" and "door," an opening cut in the house of Beth to admit wind and air after Man has made a door (Daleth) to admit himself. This wind-door was his means of receiving and perceiving Light.

A window is a vantage point for surveying all our surroundings to oversee all that goes on about us.

As a result of this supervision we are enabled to order and control our personal universe. Through the attributes of Heh, we gain both vision and supervision. Then, after having minutely examined all that appears without, we refine vision to achieve insight into the realities of creation. We penetrate its inmost nature by seeing through that which is outwardly visible.

Rather than merely looking at things about you, develop true vision by looking into them. See things as they are - not as they appear. The higher vision includes insight into man's own powers, thus becoming true perception. By watching, he has learned to see.

This is illustrated by comparative levels of vision. A child simply sees a "house"; the purchaser sees its function; the architect, its plan. The artist goes still further in his infinite pains to reproduce its image. He gazes deep into the subject of his inspection to bring out more than is usually evident, whether of beauty or intrinsic values, seeing much that is ordinarily passed over unnoticed. The study of art helps anyone improve his powers of observation.

According to the quality of our vision do we make the definition of ourselves and environment. As we see, we also make patterns which the formative power tends to bring forward into manifestation.

The Emperor is called The Onlooker, and the power of nature works because he is looking on. Moreover, because of his watchfulness, he cannot be surprised nor overwhelmed, by misfortune nor by enemies.

Qabalistically, this is called the Path of the Constituting or Measuring Intelligence "because it constitutes creation (or the substance of Creation) in pure darkness." To constitute a thing is to set it up or establish it; whereas to measure is to find its range, capacity, or extent.

When the early fathers of our country found themselves with an infant nation to be ruled and directed, one of the first important moves was to draw up the framework of regulation called a Constitution.

"To constitute" also means to ordain, or appoint. Not only are "things" set in order, but also people are appointed those places where they best fit according to measured capacity. In this work of putting affairs in order, things are set up on a solid "four-square" basis of operation.

The square diagram has long been the symbol of matter and formation, the solid foundation in building - four corners creating a state of secure establishment which will not allow the structure to topple. The builder must measure all things correctly to distinguish what is true through reason and clear vision.

The original four-letter word was the Tetragrammaton, JHVH, the Hebrew Divine Name. In Greek, *tetra* means "four," while *gramma* means "letter." The exact pronunciation of the Yod-Heh-Vav-Heh has been lost because it was so holy as to be unspeakable by any but the High Priest when he entered the Holy of Holies once each year.

After the destruction of the temple at Jerusalem within the century following Jesus' birth, the pronunciation of the Creator's Name was gradually forgotten. In Hebrew writing, the vowels are omitted and only the framework of a word is written down, so we still have only the four consonants with which the Name was spelled. It has been wrongly pronounced Jehovah; sometimes Yahweh.

The letter Heh is twice repeated in this Name; as second and fourth letter. Therefore, it denotes a very important factor in the process of Creation. In Qabalistic writings, it was said that Heh, the letter of this Key, was the letter "wherewith Creation took place," the second Heh being as offspring or daughter of the first.

He sits on a solid cube, each side a perfect square, and thus a symbol of Truth and Order. It is composed of stone; in Hebrew *ehben*. This word is a contraction of *Ab* (Father) and *Ben* (Son); therefore, stone in the Tarot is a symbol of the union of Father and Son.

This Key represents Aries, first sign of the Zodiac, which begins the fourth month of the year. Here, the Sun, which was born in darkness of winter, shows its first outward effect as Spring brings a visible resurrection of Nature from the apparent "death" of winter; that which was growing within now becomes manifest outwardly.

The Sun is exalted in Aries as shown by the gold trim of the helmet and globe, the metal of the Sun, and by the orange color of the sky, one of the colors assigned to the sun, yet composed of a blend of mental-yellow plus action-red.

The rulership of warlike Mars over Aries is evident in his metal which is used for steel armor, and his red color in the mountains, and on the helmet, which suggests that of a fireman. Red is the color used to denote fiery activity and creative energy, as well as the "red tincture" of the alchemist.

Aries is a Fire sign ruling the head which exercises control over the whole body through the brain. He is a leader and pioneer. Symbols of Aries are evident: one atop his helmet, and the ram on the cube—the Ram acting as leader of the flock of sheep.

Behind him flows the cool stream of the underlying or subconscious mind which waters his judgments with mercy, and from which he draws remembrance. This "water" gradually breaks down the fiery red rock through erosion and combines with it to form the fertile soil which can be planted for The Empress' garden. "Adam" means "red earth"; he was the first man. The red color is lowest in the spectrum, or nearest to physical density.

In his right hand is the Egyptian Ankh, a symbol of Venus and The Empress. He rules with love. It is a sign of Life, and "Eve" also means "living." It becomes here, by its color and shape, a combined symbol of Light, Life, and Love. Her color, the green of nature, like Eden, forms the footing on which his throne is established. The ten small circles on his helmet refer to the ten Sephiroth.

The emblem in his left hand is a symbol of dominion over the terrestrial forces of earth's globe, its material trend indicated by the cross on top. Four is also a symbol of the four-armed cross.

His white shield refers to the purity of Spirit, its five sides reiterating the relationship to Mars through the fifth Sphere on the Tree of Life. The double-headed eagle emblazoned on the shield suggests initiative, swift creative energy, and regeneration. The two heads of equal dignity indicate equilibrium or the balance of opposite forces.

His legs are posed again in the form of the number 4, or a cross, but the posture of his whole figure resembles the symbol for alchemical sulphur (pictured at left). That is, the triangle of the Law standing above and triumphing over the cross of the material realm. Sulphur suggests those passional fires which both tempt man to turn aside from the spiritual path, and burn the dross from his being.

He is called Sovereign Reason, the Eye of the Mind, occupying the intellectual throne. Order is achieved with the help of Reason—these being the two principal functions of this Key.

The Monarch ruling his empire is your real Self. Use this Key to strengthen the pattern of order and control in your own life. Whenever a new condition of any kind enters your life, take immediate steps to put it in its rightful place in the scheme of things and "set your affairs in order."

Remember particularly, any attempt to achieve order in your life must begin by establishing order in your thinking, and as you drop the pebble into the pool of your affairs, the widening ripples will affect every part of your life.

Put the "head" in order first as in the first commandment. You place the Godhead first in all things that all else may fall into its rightful place.

The Number Four and the Square in Symbolism

In the Zohar, it is stated that the Four Elements or the four phases of matter are the roots and source of all things both above and below.

"There are four," according to an old saying, "which take the first place in this world: man, among the creatures; the eagle among the birds; the ox among cattle; and the lion among wild beasts." In the order mentioned above, the symbols represent the four elements in combination with the four fixed signs of the zodiac. Thus, Aquarius, and Air; Scorpio, and Water; Taurus, and Earth; and Leo, and Fire.

The quaternary, or four-sided figure, was anciently called the most mysterious number, because it contains all the mysteries of nature; and the most perfect number because the root of other numbers, and of all things. It is also known as the first mathematical power, and a symbol of the Eternal and Creative Principle.

In the world of elements, there are four seasons, four winds, four directions, and the four qualities corresponding to the four elements—namely: heat, cold, moisture, and dryness.

The number Four is a symbol of terrestrial order, or orderly arrangement. It is claimed that the fourth Sephirah, Mercy, represents the first day of Creation, and the beginning of form. Four is also the Tetragrammaton, the Divine Name JHVH, whose letters correlate with the four planes of Creation.

In Revelation 21:16, the holy city was seen coming down out of heaven from God, four-square, its length the same as its breadth.

The Emperor: Key 4

Path 16
Triumphant and External Intelligence

Intuition *Sign Taurus*

Key 5

THE TEACHER
(Formerly called The Hierophant)

Letters U, V, or W   **Vav – Nail**

Revealer of Mysteries—the Voice Within.

You shall weep no more. He will surely be gracious to you at the sound of your cry; when He hears it, He will answer you. And though the Lord gives you the Bread of Adversity and the Water of Affliction, yet your Teacher will not hide Himself anymore, but your eyes shall see your Teacher. And your ears shall hear a word behind you saying, "This is the Way; walk in it." When you turn to the right or when you turn to the left. (Isaiah 30:19 – 21)

Fatherhood began with the previous Key 4 The Emperor, who exercised reason and authority to bring his flock forward into a pattern of orderly activity.

But once the mechanics have been established and things are functioning properly, the children, or nation, or individuals involved have themselves arrived at the age of reason. So now they must be taught how to function at a higher level, and their finer capacities have to be aroused with the aid of wisdom. Then does the strict father lay aside armor and helmet to put on the softer, yet tougher, vestments representing spiritual authority and peace.

As pope or guru (not of any specific religion, but simply *il papa* or spiritual father), he replaces outer command with inner rule. For the functions of this Key are Intuition and Inner Hearing, and these begin where Reason leaves off. Here the subconscious response to Reason carries development still further and enhances the results.

The word "in-tuition" means interior teaching, just as to "instruct" means to "build-in." This inner teaching goes beyond mere hunches and reaches into collective human experience so it may be called "spiritual intuition." This brings a direct perception of eternal principles resulting from the union of personal consciousness with Cosmic Consciousness.

The Teacher is in some ways a composite of all the preceding Keys, partaking of their attributes as a son takes after all his grandparents. He is one with the Self, The Fool, uses the wise arts of The Magician; has the priestly authority of The High Priestess, the love of The Empress, and the firmness of The Emperor.

Having accomplished the basic principles, he can now turn attention to higher matters. Thus, the number 5 and The Teacher act as a bridge between lower and higher—a turning point. The number 5, itself, is a half-way point in the numbers from 1 to 9. It is thus considered the number of Man himself, as the mid-point and the mediator between Nature and God. This, too, is the meaning of the five-pointed star or pentagram.

In crossing-over from one state to another, we find the idea of "bridge," or the link between that which is above and that below, and between that which is below and that above. A pope or bishop is called *pontifex*, a Latin word meaning "bridge-maker," and this term describes well the function of a priest acting as mediator between man and God.

This Key is related to Taurus, which rules the throat, while the Hebrew letter for the Key is *Vav*, meaning "hook" or "nail"—thus a link which joins together. The letter *Vav* represents any one of our letters U, V, and W.

Ecclesiastes 12 states: "Like nails firmly fixed are the collected sayings which are given by one Shepherd." And from another source we hear of "the nailing or fixing of the word." Jesus Christ was nailed to a cross. His crucifixion was the Key opening the Gates of Heaven. He linked Heaven (within) to Earth (without).

The Teacher is not limited to any one church or faith, but is a Universal Father. He represents the Inner Voice which instructs us in universal principles and becomes a connecting link between outer experience and inner Illumination. While he works on the inner plane, the instruction applies equally to that which is without.

This Key relates to the Self within, in the relationship of the Teacher and Instructor, by means of the Inner Voice. Interior hearing is the teaching of Truth which comes from within. The Teacher represents that Self which brings about at-one-ment with the Universal Being. He pours Wisdom's living sweetness into the spiritual ear that "hears."

"Hierophant," the former name of this Key, was a title given the chief officer in the Eleusinian mysteries. It means one who explains or interprets sacred rites, as "the revealer of sacred things." He is an Initiate, a Master of the Mysteries of Life, holding Keys to its hidden doctrines.

We have chosen a title more in keeping with the Teacher discipleship relationship of Universal Truth, which can be applied to any place or time. Teaching embraces all methods of imparting knowledge, such as instruction, guidance, discipline or counsel. A spiritual teacher seeks to make known and accepted these higher Truths to which he has attained, through training and direction which make use of precept, example and experience, especially the last two.

The gold and silver crossed keys indicate the union and balance of solar-positive and lunar-negative forces. These are the Keys to the Kingdom which Jesus gave Cephas, who became known as the first Christian pope.

Other symbols of union are the gray of wisdom and the coloring of pillars and background, which shows the blending of all pairs of opposites into uniformity. The crosses on hands, feet and carpet also indicate this uniting of opposites.

Venus is the planetary ruler of Taurus—the lover of beauty and "good living" and of substantial things. The Moon is exalted in this sign, as is shown by its position at the throat, or Taurus area. Other symbols of this sign appear in the design at upper corners of his throne, and the Venus symbols on the carpet are folded double so their cross is inside the circle rather than below it. Thus they become coins, a medium of exchange, part of the Taurus function, and also symbols of the element Earth.

The diamond design on the carpet represents the hardness of fixed earth, while the bull of Taurus represents Earth in its strongest and most balanced form.

Orange-red is assigned to Taurus on the color scale, and is the color of his robe and carpet. The color of opposite-sign Scorpio is edging his robe; its curving fashion suggests the Kundalini or serpent force, and also reminds us that each sign partakes somewhat of the qualities of its opposite sign. The white sash around his middle indicates the inner or spiritual path which binds his outer consciousness—a symbol of cohesion and commitment.

His two fingers uplifted, the rest concealed, imply: "I'm not telling you all at once, son; much remains to be learned." But through what is taught, you achieve growth of consciousness.

In our early impatience as students, we seek all the answers at once, in plain language, wishing nothing reserved. But one can only handle a little at a time over a long period; like food, it has to be digested and assimilated. Someone might show you all the food needed over a period of years to attain a certain growth, or give you lists and menus of it, but you couldn't eat or handle this all at once; and only the eating, with careful mastication and thorough incorporation into your structure, is of any value in your growth.

The true Teacher stands at a higher level, having learned from experience. He is supposed to know more until you reach his stature. Otherwise, what could he teach you? The Self is even more wisely conservative than a human teacher, yet never- failing when contact is real. You are told or shown just enough.

The staff symbolizes dominion of the Life-Power through the planes (cross-bars) of Nature, with the knob at the top representing the archetypal world. Similarly, his crown or turban also relates to the four worlds beginning with the Archetypal plane on top.

The two novitiates depict the children being taught, the students. 'Except ye become as a little child, ye cannot enter into the Kingdom of Heaven." Each has been garbed to represent one of the fields of endeavor cultivated in Key 1 by The Magician.

The seeker robed with roses has chosen the Path of love for humanity, and spiritual unfoldment through heartfelt activity, the hands ardently spread out to show open-heartedness, touching the keys of the Kingdom as did Peter. Yet, the passive or receptive element is indicated, as well, by his placement at left in the picture.

The other seeker is sometimes depicted with his fingertips upward in prayer, and this is the attitude of devotion and pure mindedness—the white lilies. His red robe indicates activity in this field. On their backs are yokes implying "yoga," the union of man and God in consciousness—this union being one of the major keynotes of the picture. The yokes are shaped exactly as the letter *Vav* was written in old Hebrew characters.

Their white caps cover the crown chakra, in reverence toward that to which they aspire, to become crowned with the Great Light and Mind of God. They are also a reminder to keep their thoughts pure.

In I Kings 19:12, Elijah had been told to go and stand on a mountain before the Lord. There passed by in succession a strong wind, an earthquake, and a hurricane; but the Lord was in none of these. "And after that, a still small voice"—and this proved to be the Voice of God, who then spoke to him. This also applies to Keys 16 and 17.

"Be still and know that I am God." (Psalm 46:10) We know that we must listen well to correctly hear any conversation among our associates. How much more shall we need to keep silent in order to hear a *still* small Voice speaking wisely within ourselves? You must learn to listen in order to hear; for the work of The Teacher concerns *inner* teaching.

Keys 5 and 2 have been called the Archpriest and the Archpriestess. There is a definite correlation between them. Let us glance at an older French version which depicts this similarity more obviously, and titles them *Le Pape* and *La Papesse*.

Both are shown seated between two pillars, the one on the viewer's right is gold and the other silver. Between these is drawn a red veil, hers being attached to a gold ring at the upper center of each pillar, while his is strung on a gold rod behind the pillars.

Each wears a white robe trimmed with gold, but beneath her robe shows a pale blue gown. He holds the conventional staff. Both are girded with a gold cord, and both wear a triple-tiered crown. Atop his is a golden cross, but hers bears a golden crescent moon with corners turned upward to receive. Attached to her crown is a short veil which just covers her eyes.

In her left hand is held a book, and in her right are two very large keys, one of silver and one of gold. The floor beneath her throne is of checkered black and white tiles, to show the influence of polarity or of light and darkness in alternate cycles as of day and night. They carry the same meaning as those beside The Teacher's feet in this Key.

Both of these depict the function of receiving from above. But she sits alone, taking in and recording impressions for future reference, while he holds himself receptive for the purpose of immediate transmission, and for practical as well as spiritual guidance.

Before him kneel two humble white-haired figures, in attitudes of prayer. They are simply robed, one in red wearing a skull cap, and the other in plain blue with no Cap.

The Archpriest is blessing them, but in so doing is acting not of himself, but as a mediator and channel for the Divine Blessing. He receives instructions from above, both for himself and for them.

The Teacher: Key 5

Path 17
The Disposing Intelligence

Discernment　　　　　　　　　　　　　　　　　　　*Sign Gemini*

Key 6

THE LOVERS

Letter Z   Zain – Sword

*True healing is the attainment of inner and
outer wholeness through contact with the Self.*

In order to give the first man of Earth a proper mate, God separated Adam for a time from a portion of his own being so that the two complementary parts could come fully to understand and cooperate, each with the other. Meanwhile their Creator would fill the gap between, until that time when they should be again joined together in Himself.

Love is a balancing force which brings all things into harmony and holds back nothing, because it is all good. One must love divinely and not just "fall" in love. There is no darkness in divine love, nor in selfless personal love.

This can only happen when our sights are turned to that which is above and we are hearkening to the voice of the Lord, or of His Holy Emissary—in this case Raphael, the Archangel of Healing and of the element Air, of Prana and the Cosmic Life-Breath.

Raphael's name means "God is the Healer." This also implies that our healing, or our health, depends on the harmonizing of our consciousness with that of the Cosmic.

In this Key is represented the zodiacal sign Gemini, whose ruler is Mercury. Mercury is the planet of Mind, and we know how important is our state of mind in relation to general health, and that a drastic change of mind can change the state of wellbeing—this being within our prerogative of choice.

In a state of primal innocence Adam and Eve are dwelling in the original Garden of Delight ("delight" or "pleasure" being the translation of the word Eden). Innocence is never ashamed; they are open and clear with God and with each other.

There are no shadows or secret places in their consciousness, much like children, without guile. When mankind was in his primeval state, he was obedient as a child to his elders. The person who is obliged to do the will of another holds no guilt nor weight of decision. But when he reaches maturity, he is beset with choices and then becomes like a god, in that he is free to choose. But he also has to pay for his choices.

Have you ever thought, as a child: "I'll be glad when I grow up to be my own boss, and do what I want to do?" But on coming of age you took, along with freedom, the responsibility for your very wants. Innocence was gone, and so was Eden's childish delight. You had become like a god, adult and responsible.

The Tree of Knowledge of Good and Evil stands behind Eve. The fruits of the five senses are shown thereon, as yet, untasted. The serpent is lifted up for healing.

She represents the subconscious mind—that area of underlying and automatic consciousness which is most susceptible to subtle insinuations. In fact, our subconscious minds are more readily influenced in this indirect way than by definite statements.

Because of the mistake in tasting this fruit of the senses, which darkened the mind with confusion so that the body had to be covered, man could not, in that condition of mind, be allowed to eat of the Tree which would give eternal life, but was driven out lest he remain forever in an unevolved, confused state.

Man asked for, and received, the doubtful privilege of having to decide every moment of life if a thing is good or bad; if he should laugh or cry; if he should give or take. In original innocence, he needed give no thought. The fruit of the Tree of Life was being guarded and saved until the day when man would become a regenerated, spiritual being, a fit citizen for the New Jerusalem. This is the "Happy Ending" of the Bible in the last chapter, returning to man what he had lost in the book of Genesis.

> "On either side of the river, the Tree of Life, with its twelve kinds of fruit, yielding its fruit each month, and the leaves of the Tree were for the healing of the nations. There shall no more be anything accursed, but the throne of God and the Lamb shall be in it, and His servants shall worship Him." (Revelation 22: 2-3)

The leaves of the Tree of Life shall be for healing (mentioned above) and Key 6 denotes healing, as does the Archangel Raphael.

Whether there be any correlation between the fact that fig leaves were used to cover the shame of Adam and Eve, and later, Jesus cursed another fig tree because it bore only leaves, we do not know. But He did say: "May no fruit ever come from you again." And it is good to think that He was somehow deleting the mistake of Adam and Eve with their fig leaves and clearing the way for the Tree of Life with its healing leaves promised later.

It is clear that God did not want to perpetuate the consciousness which divides everything and categorizes it good or bad. So, He drove them forth to work very hard, and earn their own way, and eventually, purge their inmost beings and bring them once more to God—not in shame, but in true repentance and total dedication, having experienced both sides of the coin.

The Hebrew letter *Zain* is assigned this Key. Its meaning is "sword." A sword cleaves apart, or splits in half. Eve was the only helpmeet found for Adam equal to him, able to stand by his side, because she was of his own kind: "Flesh of his flesh, and bone of his bone."

In the former Key 5 The Teacher, *Vav* was the nail which joined things together—the cohesive factor. But Key 6 is called The Disposing Intelligence, because the figures are "posed apart," or cut asunder. When a part of man was taken from himself, he was able to stand back and look at the other half.

The sense of smell and the function of discrimination are assigned to this Key. "Properties are discovered by the nose," and through smell, one is able to discriminate or choose correctly in the positive meaning of the word. The sword also refers to this act of right discrimination—not as against anything, but as we must choose at each crossroad which way to pursue, "cutting things right down the middle," as it were.

An ancient version of this Key pictured a young man on the Path struggling between which of two women, called Vice and Virtue, he should choose. The angel of Justice flew overhead aiming an arrow in this battle between passion and conscience, showing that whatever the choice, the consequences would be just. Thus, Zain relates to the powers of choice. The sword is also a symbol of the Word, and of the Air element.

Gemini is ruled by Mercury, who in mythology carried the caduceus or wand of miracles, a staff with two serpents twined about, which is still used as a symbol of medicine. Moses was also directed by God to "make a fiery serpent and set it on a pole, and everyone who is bitten, when he sees it, shall live."

This happened in the wilderness as Moses was leading the people through very difficult times. When they complained against God and Moses, fiery serpents were sent to bite some of them, who then died (Numbers 21:5). So Moses made a bronze serpent according to instructions from on High, and set it on a pole, so if a serpent bit any man, he could look at the bronze serpent and live.

In another time, Jesus said, "And as Moses lifted up the serpent in the wilderness, so must the Son of Man be lifted up that whosoever believes in him may have eternal life." (John 3:14)

The Lovers: Key 6

This is a curious statement, but in each case, it was the lifting up from the ground which symbolized the conquering and control of these subtle forces that they might be used for good. The controlled "serpent power" became the means of healing.

The forces within man—the subtle underlying powers when lifted above the earthly, sensual level, also become a power for bringing the individual into that balance needed to heal the ills which his uncontrolled state has caused.

The serpent also symbolizes the Kundalini fire, which at first deludes man into temptation then, when overcome, helps to deliver him from evil.

The sun is shown here as a "golden force," rather than white, to represent the physical source of energy and life—the visible body of the invisible spiritual Sun.

The angel's wings are red to denote right action, while the violet robe blends the red of action with the blue of mental substance (blue plus red equals violet). The angel rests horizontally on a cloud showing that man's spiritual powers are not fully developed and that until they are, these must remain partially hidden.

His hair is of tri-colored flaming energy, and at center, above the forehead, is shown a feather-tiara of shining gold, which acts as a focus of attention in healing concentration.

Gemini is the sign of the twins, of duality. Yet, all pairs of opposites complement, and thus, complete each other. Polarities are all two extremes of one thing as heat and cold are the extremes, or two ends, of temperature, and past and future are two extremes of time.

The alchemical function of this Key is Fixation, the establishment of firm awareness of the true relation and function of the alchemical principles which are symbolized as mercury, sulphur, and salt. The element air predominates, being of middle nature between the fire of calcination and the salt of earth.

Fixation is the stability of perfect equilibrium, the work of Mercury, The Magician. It involves perfect balance of the solar and lunar forces of the two sides of the human body.

The conscious mind has to look to the subconscious for guidance because the Cosmic Mind does not speak directly to the outer awareness, but must reach from Its own high level through the medium of the inner awareness which, in turn, translates these impulses into conscious thought. Therefore, it is important that subconsciousness reflect the true knowledge from the plane of the Absolute, seeking guidance ever from the Mind of God and his angelic messenger, and never from the crawling, creeping forces of animal instinct which are on a lower level than man's own. Therefore, her gaze is ever upward.

The Lovers: Key 6

Path 18
Intelligence of House and Influence
Receptivity-Will   *Sign Cancer*

Key 7

THE CHARIOT

Letter Ch **Cheth – Fenced Field**

The body of man, solidified out of the "chaos" of the four elements, became his vehicle, its reins being handed over to the driver—Self. Thus were incarnated the higher principles of the nature of Man. The four pillars of the Universe represent the four directions of Space, and the four elements which he has conquered can be used as supports. A ring around each represents the Ultimate Enclosure of all things within the circle of Spirit.

Certain Qabalistic teachings of the Zohar are sometimes called "the Work of the Chariot." The Chariot of JHVH which appeared to Ezekiel was said to have wheels likened to "whirlwinds of Fire," and to indicate the entire solar system as the Chariot of God whose wheels represent the orbits of planets.

For this reason, the wheels in this version are colored orange, to suggest the fiery energy of Spirit as the cause of their revolving motion. Jupiter, which has to do with the circulation of blood as well as with planetary cycles, is represented by the Wheel of Key 10, and is also the planet exalted in Cancer.

The canopy is colored a deep night-sky blue, the color sometimes used for the Sphere of Understanding on the Tree of Life. From this canopy shine the stars to show that the energy of celestial forces are continually beaming down, affecting every individual. Though they only appear nightly overhead, their influence actually surrounds us at all times, on all sides.

The Charioteer represents exterior conquest of all planes, particularly the mental sciences, the earlier initiations, and triumph of mind over matter. It is his victory over the senses which has made him a king. "He who overcomes shall inherit the Crown of the Kingdom."

The Crown he is wearing shows three pentagrams, to symbolize man's dominion over the three lower planes of nature through proper use of speech: the animal, vegetable, and mineral kingdoms. The crown is of gold to represent the solar forces involved.

The Hebrew letter-word for this Key, *Cheth*, translates literally as "enclosure," or "fenced field," and equals Ch, or audible H.

A fence is built around a house or field to establish its rightful boundary lines and to permit intensive cultivation therein. Similarly one builds the atmosphere around his own body as far out as his personal influence extends. Within any "fenced" area of influence, one plants or builds that which he wishes to produce for the good of himself or others. Cheth's work also encloses and protects the walled city behind him—a multiplication of the efforts of The Magician, who built the first house.

All fences are temporary, artificial boundary lines, for land extends undivided beneath them as it always did before they were built, and always will when they are gone. The very nature of a fence necessitates that one day all must be broken down in order to do away with the false notion of separateness, and so that we may recognize and unite with the One God. The temporary fence makes possible some specialization, as in gardening, and helps keep out alien influences while the crop is tended and its growth nurtured along.

The particular function of this Key is Speech. Speech can be likened to a fenced area of Sound—thought brought forth into audibility, controlled, defined, and directed.

Whereas Beth, The Magician, using thought, made his personality-house a channel for divine power, here Cheth goes one step further to become driver of his vehicle and manipulator of thought into speech. He has led forth to victory the mental processes and has become king over and through his own mind, earning the right to be called Master of the Temple.

The sphinxes represent the senses—half-lion and half-woman—which always pose riddles man must solve correctly or perish in the battle of mastery over lower forces. These also refer to hidden or occult forces, and when controlled they help pull man's chariot.

The questions posed by the sphinxes relate to mysteries of Nature; to answer them at last and pass by successfully is to obtain for oneself the right to immortality. The Egyptian Sphinx was masculine in front and feminine behind to include the dual wholeness of one Being in one person. Pharaohs sometimes wore the tail of a lion or cow to show this.

The lines of control used by the driver are the invisible reins of Mind. Here they have checked the animal instinct of the subconscious and have it under direction, while also partaking of her higher, purer elements shown by the silver crescents on his shoulders. Like the pure silver of heavenly "water," Self is shown here springing up from his stone encasement, as water rises in a well. "A well of water springing up unto eternal life." (John 4:14)

Cancer, as the first water sign of the Zodiac, represents the place of initiative waters, the beginning of a rushing stream. A mountain spring runs rapidly down to water the fields below; so from the Great Within of our own personal temple, the powers flow down into daily experience.

The energy referred to is likened to "water," in that it ebbs and flows and has a purifying aspect; for all forms are held in suspension within it, or are dissolved therein.

Until now, the waters of subconsciousness have been seen in their natural state, undifferentiated, the stream of consciousness flowing quietly in the background.

But here, a fence is built, and the subconscious substances are enclosed, even as a well may be encased with tiles, or a fountain with marble, that the water may be used and its flow controlled. Thus, one may have use of pure water in his own abode.

Cancer is the sign of this Key—the protective and parental sign which shelters and nurtures the younger or the weaker until they have gained the strength of independence. Cancer is ruled by the Moon, whose corresponding metal is silver and whose element is water. Its symbol is usually a crab, and this shape is suggested by the brass breastplate, a Venus-metal referring to the protective power of imagination.

The square on his chest, with its three *Tav's*, is at the center of four pillars like the Self at the center of the Cube of Space.

The lunar masks on his shoulders compare with the facial expressions of the two sphinxes, the one indicating a positive or waxing crescent and the other a negative or waning one. There is also reference in this to the pillars of polarity in Key 2 and all pairs of opposites.

His belt, slanted like the plane of the ecliptic, refers to the encirclement of the zodiac and to the boundaries of Time, while the whole celestial sphere of the starry heavens serves as his canopy. Symbols of magic cover his skirt.

Cypress trees in the background show the imaginative nature of most Cancer persons, and the Venusian growth influence of this fertile and productive sign.

This Key refers both to the womb and to the birthplace of a universe, as intimated by the abounding celestial symbols.

The gray stone enclosure of the chariot signifies that he is a Son of the Father. *Ab* (Father) plus *Ben* (Son) equals *Ehben*, the Hebrew word for "stone." This is again a cornerstone of the foundation which has been a stumbling block for the unworthy or unwise.

The red symbol on the white shield is a Hindu symbol, material and active, called the *lingam-yoni*, and signifies the continuous process of creation and preservation in the universe. The diamond shows light and brilliance manifested in heaven and earth. The knob below is manifested earth and the disk is a land between.

His gold and silver staff refers to the uniting principle, the silver-negative moon and the gold-positive figure eight at its top depicting solar forces.

The golden solar disk with its blue wings represents the Sun, with the moist blue atmosphere which brings its rays to earth; or the old Sun god Ra, and his domination of air and space. Wings denote spiritual mission and upliftment. "The Sun of Righteousness shall rise with healing in his wings." (Malachi 4:2)

The grail, wafted in by the dove of peace and the Holy Spirit, is sometimes called the "Source of Illumination." It has traditionally been described as pure amethyst, relating to Jupiter's exaltation in Cancer, but we have used a sacramental cup fashioned of gold, with silver trim and an amethyst band. A reference to Melchizedek (Genesis 14:18-24) is suggested here.

Seven is a number of mastery and poise—a most sacred number composed of three plus four, which is much used in all religions. The Latin *septem* means seven, while *septum* means "enclosure" or "wall," emphasizing its connection with the letter Cheth.

Seven has earned the right to rest; for the labors of the Sixth Day are done. Actually, it is on the seventh *plane* that God rests; He is always working and resting at the same time.

Man has found it both wise and healthful to rest on the seventh day, or Sabbath. His vacation is called a sabbatical leave. The temporary cessation of outer activity brings not only Strength (see Key 8) for the morrow, but also an increase of activity on the inner level, and it is in this quiet space that the still small voice can be heard.

Cheth moves beyond listening and speaks. Through utterance, he reproduces in sound what was heard in silence; for Breath produces Speech when cultivated and mastered. Speech is the function of this Key. This correlates with the religious services of the traditional Sabbath where physical work is temporarily stilled and man listens to the spoken words of God and His prophets, where inner Truths are outwardly expounded.

These religious services, when correctly performed, reiterate the universal principles of the heavens.

While Key 7 represents a grade of attainment through victory over opposing forces, it is not yet the ultimate attainment of the mountain top, or of God-Realization, any more than going to church to preach or listen to the Sunday sermon represents spiritual attainment. Here is rather a plateau near the mountain top—a place to sit and rest before continuing to climb, with the end in view and success assured.

Ideas are carried into the field of consciousness by the vehicle of the subconscious mind. The chariot is a movable "house," or house on wheels, the vehicle which carries us wherever we will go, having restored the Creator to His Throne.

To quote the Bhagavad-Gita: "The Self is the Rider in the chariot of the body, of which the senses are horses, and the mind the reins." Their field is the universe.

While Cheth builds a fence about each portion to define the boundaries and close out inimical influences; he simultaneously closes in the desired area for more concentrated observation and use of that which he wishes to retain.

But the day of maturity inevitably comes when these fences are seen from a higher perspective, not as barriers to freedom, but merely as tools used for a time, after which one must expand outward to prove his Strength.

A writer may close his door and sit in a small space nearly motionless to concentrate all his energy and attention on a specific work which must be undiluted with other ideas. But when it is finished, he opens the door and goes out to other things. The limitation has accomplished its end, and the fence is removed.

The Chariot: Key 7

Path 19
Intelligence of Secret of Spiritual Activities

Suggestion *Sign Leo*

Key 8

STRENGTH

Letter T   **Teth – Snake**

Thou shalt love the Lord, thy God, with all thy heart, and with all thy strength, and with all thy mind. (Matthew 22:37)

Key 8 is the octave of The Magician; that is, returning to the same idea at a different level. They appear in similar roles, each with the horizontal eight above the head to show the achievement of power and control.

Mercury, the mental magician, used the tools of the four elements. In Key 6, he achieved health through mental balance, and in Key 7, was able to cooperate with Self in controlling the senses.

But the beast depicted here is an inner and living force, which in its wild, uncontrolled state has too often proved stronger than man's mind. It was then the "ravening beast" which tore the vitals with destructive passion, whether of "love," anger, or despair.

Here the time has come to deal with and control this powerful inner agent: Fire in its natural state cannot be allowed to get out of bounds lest it destroy. Yet it is one of mankind's greatest blessings for simple warmth or cooking, even to the eternal flame burning on an altar as the symbol of Spirit.

The direct application of mind cannot be used to control this beast, but a subtler approach from the refined part of our nature, the subconscious mind, is required to achieve this control. The woman depicts that area of consciousness which lies below the surface of direct awareness, and begins to take hold and go to work to change the course of Nature when its own nature has been fully purified and patterned.

This is not done by afflicting and mortifying the flesh, neither by destroying the desire nature. But the fragrant red roses of acceptable desires are so chosen and woven together that these form an infinite pattern—a figure eight twined about both woman and lion in the symbol of infinity ∞ the endless cyclic flow. The tie of love is meant to be constructive.

Red is an active color, here both activating right desire and the desire for right action, in an artfully persuasive way, much as a burly athlete might respond to the refinement of a beautiful gentle woman.

She has taken the roses from The Magician's garden, depending on his earlier work to cultivate this beauty; and it is his patient attention and work which has brought forward the refinement of her own nature.

By taming this great power, lifting it above the animal level and making it submissive, this remains on call when needed, and can be used or called forth to willing action, through Love.

"We love because He first loved us" (John 4:19), and this makes many wish to give their lives back to Him who so fully exemplified perfect love.

Love is a great source of Strength. People are both inspired and empowered in this state to do things far beyond the scope of their normal activity.

Key 8 represents the zodiacal sign Leo (The Lion), physically a representative of the heart and the backbone. Courage is an attribute of Leo, the word deriving from the Latin *cor*, for "heart." But in slang terms, we say that a person has a great deal of "backbone" when he acts bravely.

The backbone in occultism is the channel for a secret fire called the Astral Light, Cosmic Electricity, or the "Secret of all Spiritual Activities." More commonly, you have heard it called the Kundalini, or serpent force. This force lies dormant in the average man and stirs to wakefulness when the individual begins to unfold spiritually and has gained the necessary mental self-control depicted in Key 7.

If aroused before proper spiritual development, it leads to destructive and dangerous tendencies, and should never be wakened by effort, but should be allowed to unfold by natural stages. ("Let sleeping dogs lie.") The inner spiritual consciousness knows when the time is right, so this becomes a labor of consciousness.

The form of the letter *Teth*, which translates as "snake," is shown in the shape of a coiled serpent. A more ancient form of the letter depicted a snake coiled in circular form, the circle enclosing a cross. This brings to mind Jesus' statement that he must be lifted up as Moses lifted the serpent in the wilderness, in order to draw all men to him.

The unregenerate serpent force was made to crawl on its belly for seducing Eve. But the first chapter of Revelation says that in the New Jerusalem, there shall no more be anything accursed. The lifted-up serpent becomes a symbol of healing. The force of the lion-heart, tamed, is a power for good.

In occultism, the serpent force is sometimes interchangeable with the symbol of the lion; at other times, between lion and eagle, Leo and Scorpio, and their respective, yet similar energies.

The unregenerate lion is the serpent which must be lifted up; then with the raising of this natural force to a higher, controlled use, the lion is tamed, and the uplifted serpent force becomes symbolized as an eagle.

The lion itself had three forms according to the old alchemists. Those were: (1) the unripe, or "green" lion of man's unmodified animal or desire nature, (2) then came the red lion with its fiery Mars force controlled and ripened by spiritual progression, and (3) there was the old lion, or the radiant energy called "old" because it has always been.

The Uraeus, or royal serpent attached to the very front of pharaohs' crowns, is a sacred symbol of Egypt, and serpents have long been used to show wisdom—more specifically secrets of the wise, not given to the unready in whose hands they might have proved dangerous. Their vibratory motion also signified the motion of universal energies; and their self-renewal, through shedding old skins for new, symbolized immortality.

Leo is a kingly sign, as the lion is called King of Beasts. The sun is its ruler and gold its metal. The tribe of Judah, from which Jesus came, had the lion as its symbol; Judah means "praised."

Most of the ancients worshipped sun gods of one form or another under various names. Egyptian priests sometimes wore lion robes in their ceremonies, and sometimes the solar orb was drawn with rays resembling a lion's mane. Again, the crowns of kings were originally made to represent the solar disk with the points as its rays.

Eight is a number mystically referred to Christ. There is a suggestion in this Key of the succession of signs of the zodiac from Leo, the lion to Virgo, the Virgin.

The fact that the surroundings are so natural verify the nature of the forces involved. In the background, the mountain shows a degree of attainment, plus the presence of mental energy in the yellow sky.

The wreath of the Lady of Teth is like that worn by The Empress except that flowers have developed among the leaves to show that forces of organic life have moved that much nearer to fruition.

Taste and digestion are the functions attributed to this Key. Indeed the temptation of Eve came through tasting.

When the observations coming from The Magician of mind are true and constructive, the subconscious will eventually take over automatic control of the sub-human processes of nature. Taming a lion is not a natural thing which happens without effort, but this work results in the development of great power and force. You are the ruler both of your own vehicle, and your own personal kingdom.

"In quietness and confidence shall be your Strength." (Isaiah 30)

Strength: Key 8

Path 20
The Intelligence of Will

Response *Sign Virgo*

Key 9

THE HERMIT

Letter I, J or Y   **Yod – Hand**

*All things are included in Yod,
wherefore it is called the Father of all.*

Only now, when control has been established over the beast of animal nature, can one go on toward the summit of attainment.

Nine is the number which stands for completion or attainment. The ninth month is September of the sign of Virgo, represented in this Key.

Here, The Hermit completes the building work begun by The Magician in Key 1—The Magician representing Mercury, the planet of mental awareness. Mercury rules both Gemini and Virgo, but Virgo is the sign of its exaltation so that here he finds his highest expression, or the perfection of his purpose, as far as he can go *consciously*.

He has used the staff, a symbol of the Kundalini, the serpent power, Will, and Fire to help in his climb. It is colored brown, suggesting the raising up of the earthly nature, while its seven knobs suggest the seven mystic centers along the spine.

A mountain has the shape of a triangle, a three-sided figure. Symbolically this is the element Fire. The mind must climb to its peak aided by the staff of Will, and by the Light of the lantern. The lantern is composed of two interlaced triangles representing the Star of David, the "beloved." The Hermit is lighting the Way for others with the symbol of "as above, so below."

The lantern is of reflective silver, which helps to magnify and radiate the gold, and give a brighter light at night. This is the Light begotten of Union with the Divine—the triangle again representing man's consciousness lifting its apex as high as it can go, where it meets and draws down the triangle representing the consciousness of God so that, as they unite, universal consciousness is born within the individual.

This becomes a Light in him, wherewith he can help lead others upward by the same Way, and he becomes as Jesus advised, not a hidden flame, but a lamp set upon its stand, and gives light like a city on a hill (Matthew 5:15-16).

This is no common achievement, and therefore, he stands at this point alone. But even if a crowd were about him, he still must stand in solitude at this point on the Way and go through these experiences alone; for they are inner attainments which can be shared with no one but God.

Numerically, Zero represents the Source, and Nine the goal. Here at the end of his endeavors, having gone as far as Mind can reach, he stands just at the threshold of inner planes, of the beyond, as one stands on the stage in front of curtains about to open; for the end of every cycle marks the beginning of another.

The number 9 is the square of 3 (being 3 times 3); therefore, it represents the completion or perfection of those things represented by 3. The number 3 has been revered in many faiths as a divine number, representing in Christianity the Sacred Trinity of Father, Son, and Holy Spirit.

The number 2 simply creates a polarity or rhythm where force can travel back and forth, but 3 establishes a continuity whereby force can flow around and back to the starting point, and, as a triangle can be fitted inside a circle, the line continues around.

The Hermit: Key 9

Nine is the number of the circumference of every circle (360 degrees: 3 + 6 + 0 9). There are nine rays extending from The Hermit's lantern, in accordance with a Cabalistic teaching which says, "When he is conformed, he produces nine lights...."

The number 9 was somewhat feared by the ancients since it was the final digit and, therefore, presaged changes involving the unknown. Its form is rather like that of the generative egg from whose lower side seems to flow the spirit of life. (The number six is just reversed; the egg with an up-reaching aspiration.)

Virgo is the sixth sign of the zodiac, whereas Gemini is the sixth month and the sixth Key of Tarot. Both are ruled by Mercury; both are concerned with healing.

The hands come under the rulership of Gemini and of Raphael, the Archangel of Mercury and of healing, as shown in Key 6. The messenger of the gods, Mercury, in ancient times was depicted carrying a caduceus, still used as a healing symbol by the medical profession.

The Hebrew letter *Yod* of Key 9 corresponds to I, J, or Y in English, but the word *Yod* means "hand" in the sense of the open, or creative, Hand of God extended as in blessing. It refers more to the abstract than to the active and, like the left hand, more to openness and fair-dealing than to skill or craft. It specifically implies the hand as the delicate organ of Touch. Here man "touches" the heaven worlds and achieves union through contact with that Above.

Ancient Egyptian hieroglyphs for this letter pictured a hand outstretched. Masters and Adepts may be considered as the Hands of God.

Since the zodiacal sign for this Key is Virgo, ruling health, we may also designate Yod as the Healing Hand. The laying on of hands in healing permits spiritual forces to move through and effect the transformation which often appears miraculous.

Here again we must have previously accomplished the lesson of Key 8; for successful healing of self or others necessitates the beast of emotions under perfect control. Health demands equilibrium and right thinking, and proper channeling of the powerful energies within.

The will to live is one of the most important factors in bringing a person through a crucial health situation, or the will to work, or the will to walk—some objective which makes it worthwhile to go on, not to give up.

Fittingly, The Intelligence of Will is the Qabalistic assignment of this 20th Path of the Tree of Life. It is important to set aside personal self-will as unreal, knowing there is but One Will in reality—the Will of God; and as we function in it, we achieve peace within ourselves. "The Will of God includes Wisdom and His Wisdom is His Will."

The influence of this Path on the Tree flows downward from the grade of Exempt Adept to that of Lesser Adept. As Exempt Adept, he has already freed himself from obligation to the lower worlds, but has chosen to remain there for the time being in order to draw upward, by his example, the mass of people below.

The letter *Yod*, fashioned like a small flame, is the basic component of most of the twenty-two letters of the Hebrew alphabet, which was sometimes called the "flame alphabet," or square Hebrew, and is believed to have been developed during the exile of the Hebrews in Chaldea and to have carried with it some Chaldean derivatives of ancient wisdom teachings. In some of the other Keys, we see Yods dropping down like flames from heaven.

The Qabalah states: "Yod is above all, and with Him is none other associated." This is personified in the life of a Hermit devoted to God. "Hermit" is a better term here than recluse, suggesting the association with Hermes.

Yod is the first letter of the Tetragrammaton or unpronounceable Name of God, spelled JHVH. The omitting of vowels, after the manner of written Hebrew, caused its pronunciation to become forgotten with time.

With the first letter "J" (Y or I) is depicted the beginning of creation and of all things manifest. It is said: "The Word is the first-begotten, not the first-created, Son of God. "

Yod is called: The animating Spirit of Fire; the Generative Principle; the Creative Energy of the Deity represented as a point, and that point as the center of the circle of unmanifested Deity; the Absolute Who has no name. It is given the meaning of the Divine Energy, manifested as Light, creating the Universe.

> "The Cause of Causes made ten numerations, and called the Source of Spring "Kether" (Corona, the Crown), in which the idea of circularity is involved, for there is no end to the outflow of Light; and therefore, He called this, like Himself, endless—even as the Zero is endless."

> "For this also, like Him, has no similitude or configuration, nor any vessel or receptacle wherein it may be contained."

> "After thus forming the Crown, He constituted a certain small receptacle, the letter Yod, and filled it from that Source. And this is called the Fountain gushing with Wisdom. Manifested in this, He called Himself Wise, and the vessel He called Chokmah, or Wisdom."

> "Chokmah is not absolute Wisdom of Itself, but is wise by means of Binah, understanding, wherein He fills Himself as from a reservoir, and without which He would be dry and unintelligent."

The cap of The Hermit is shaped like a Yod and colored blue. This blue is in remembrance of benevolent Chesed, the Sephirah from which this Path flows toward the Sun imitating the Cosmic Process of meditation.

The darkness of the background of this Key represents the inner, hidden or subconscious field of Divine Operation. Our contact with the

One is an interior contact just as our most important transformations are those occurring below the level of conscious awareness, even though they are the outgrowth of conscious effort.

The heights seem cold, dark and abstract to observers, but this ice refers to subconscious substance, the "water" which has crystallized.

The gray cloak designates the Wisdom which keeps him warm, while at the same time, for their own protection, concealing the mysteries from the gaze of those unprepared.

He shows the virginity of one who has become virginal through inner purity, willing service and mastery over mind, emotion and matter. He has "lifted up" the serpent powers and lighted his lamp with their oil—the wise virgins at the bridal door.

All great avatars, as the Christ within oneself, are said to be born of a virgin in the dark cave of the House of Bread (Bethlehem). For here the Life-Power "weaves the vesture" or a finer vehicle through which one eventually becomes aware of his union with God.

Virgo is the sign of work and service, as well; and persons born with the Sun positioned here (ideally) show a special readiness and willingness to work and serve, being diligent and meticulous. The secret of Virgo's purity is that at its best, it acts above the level of desire—without the shadow of self between.

The magical secret of Will lies in perfect obedience to Divine Will discovering our true place in nature; then do we enter into freedom, power and happiness. This requires constant practice of remembering that one's personal life is guided directly by the Higher Intelligence. One must be open and receptive—not only daily, but hourly—to the influx of Spirit from above.

The Hermit: Key 9

Path 21
The Rewarding Intelligence

Rotation   Planet Jupiter

Key 10

THE WHEEL OF FORTUNE

Letter K **Kaph – Grasping Hand**

The eleventh letter of the Hebrew alphabet is called the Path of Rewarding Intelligence of those who seek. This tallies with its planet Jupiter, the royal benefic and most expansive of planets.

Kaph is the Hebrew letter of this Key and it means the "grasping hand," or the cupped palm of the hand. It is a hand of holding or receiving, and being a "double letter" in the Hebrew alphabet, it represents the pair of opposites of Wealth and Poverty. The ancient pictorial glyph of the letter K showed a cupped hand extended as though to receive, while the clasped hand was also a symbol used by Pythagoras to represent the sacred number 10 in which all previous numbers were contained.

Ten is the number of the Lights of Emanation, or Sephiroth, on the Qabalistic Tree of Life. To quote from the ancient *Book of Formation:* "Ten are the numbers out of Nothing—not nine; not eleven. Ponder on this, render it evident, and lead the Creator back to His throne again. "

Ten is called the most perfect number because it includes the Unit which created all, and the Zero which symbolizes matter and chaos and from which all emerged.

The Psalmist (139: 9) says: "If I take the wings of the morning, and dwell in the uttermost parts of the sea, even there Thy hand shall lead me, and Thy right hand shall hold me." Truly He has the "whole world in His hand. "

On the lower levels of spiritual evolution, we seek "things," and consider ourselves fortunate or unfortunate to the extent that we are able to attract those objects most agreeable to bodily comfort or pleasure, forgetting that the body is a disposable vehicle for temporary use—like an automobile. Such "things" are not harmful to us as long as we keep them in their correct place, but they must remain secondary in importance, being mere tools, not out goal. They must never possess us.

In climbing the path of spiritual attainment, we slowly grasp some grains of Truth and, bit by bit, ponder these things and sometimes try them out. After many lifetimes of seeking, gaining skill, growing, and learning the great Realities (usually the hard way), comprehension finally comes, and we take firm hold of these truths to make them our own. This is the true Grasp of Kaph. Then we know that the important thing is not to have, but to be. "I am that I am."

This gives the perspective of the sphinx at the top of the wheel who is exempt from its revolutions, having overcome and gained the great summit. But let us look again for a moment at the wheel, from the level of the material-minded.

Such a one would gamble all in a game of chance, a turn of the wheel, trusting to make a "fortune" thus. He would make a new beginning, but a false one, with money as his object. And what of tomorrow's wheel? One must not remain tied to this, but seek the immortal reward of the greater Quest.

We find the true wheel as represented here based on the orderly, cyclical movements of the heavenly bodies, and all the laws of the universe. The planets rotate on their axes, each at its own speed, and circle the sun in a steady, orderly way, perfectly timed, yet each has a different Time system all its own.

Each cycle depends on the revolving of some sphere or other back to its starting point. Day depends on the earth's rotation, one complete turn on its axis. Years and seasons depend on the earth's orbit in a large circle, an ellipse around the sun, and back to its starting point.

The sun also moves within the vaster circle of the zodiac, carrying along with it all its planets that not one gets out of place or time. For the sun's energy encircles his own, holding them as in his hand, and keeping all in balance through gravity and mutual attraction. There is always a return to the starting point, with this addition—the rising scale of evolution necessitates that the cycle of motion keep spiraling upward.

Even the ordinary wheel, which gave civilization a great forward movement when attached to a vehicle, does not turn round and round in a stationary place, but each turn carries the vehicle further ahead, and this is the means of progress.

Key 0 The Fool, was assigned the planet Uranus, grandfather of the gods, whose name meant "heaven." When The Fool came down into manifestation, his symbols were those of inner and primary principles. But 10 adds "one" to "zero" and, having ascended again to heaven, he is renamed Jupiter, the sky-god.

Nine has been reduced to 0 and "Chaos," but with the added components gained from earthly experience of Name and Form. This return to "zero" is above the level of "nine" on the next floor up. This so-called chaos is very orderly, however, and filled with energy and force, nothing static there. In this heavenly turn of the wheel we stand at a brand new start with no personal knowledge of outcome, but all is in perfect order, held in the Hand of God. He knows.

It is interesting to note that our Lord grew up in Galilee, a Hebrew name which translated means "wheel, revolution," or "revolution of a wheel," and in India this word is associated with the life centers either of a world or an individual. In fact, the word chakra means "wheel."

A certain Tibetan wheel depicts the basic beliefs of Lamaism in reincarnation. The endless circumference indicates immortality—the six spokes symbolize six divisions of life and religion.

The Tibetans also used a prayer wheel consisting of written prayers stuffed into a wheel; then as the wheel spun round and

Jewels of the Wise

round, each turn presented the prayer. Larger wheels were used for community prayers.

Our wheel here has eight spokes—the number eight being a symbol of solar energy. This radiates out from the hub at the center which represents pure Idea, or Spirit. Here, at the hub, the central point, is the beginning of the whole creative process.

The middle section, where the eight spokes meet, shows the alchemical symbols representing the three major principles of:

Sulphur	🜍	Passion and Activity
Mercury	☿	Mind and Consciousness
Salt	⊖	Inertia and Matter

At the bottom of the wheel is the symbol for dissolution (dissolving to start over): ♒, which is also the symbol for Aquarius.

The outer circle contains actual letters, both Hebrew and Latin, the JHVH or the Hebrew Divine Name interspersed with the Latin word ROTA meaning "wheel." Spelled the other way around, it says Tora, or Law. And in still another way, Tarot.

The four "worlds" are represented here: (1) the Archetypal world by the center point; (2) the Creative world by the inner circle; (3) the next circle shows the Formative world; (4) and the outermost circle, the Material world.

Following this through in another way, we may say: first, the central point represents Idea in Spirit; then radiating out is Light of solar Energy; next the alchemical principles of the elements; and finally the power of the Word (in letters).

THE SQUARING OF THE CIRCLE

Not until after the Word of Creation has been spoken does one arrive at actual form—first with the symbolic forms around the wheel and finally the dense form of actual living creatures, as the whirling force of energy radiates outward from circle to square. The "squaring of the circle" brings the inmost principle into the dense matter of actual form.

The four creatures in the corners of the Wheel represent the four elements in their densest state of solidified matter, all being symbols of the "fixed" signs of the Zodiac.

The fixation of the principle of *Air* is shown by the Man, symbol of Aquarius. The fixed principle of *Fire* is shown by the Lion, symbol of Leo. The fixed principle of *Water* is shown by the Eagle, symbol of Regenerated Scorpio. The fixed principle of *Earth* is shown by the Ox, symbol of Taurus.

The yellow serpent, Typhon, depicts the serpent power of Teth descending. It represents the involution of the radiant energy or light vibration of the Cosmos into the field of form.

The jackal-headed creature, the Egyptian Thoth or Hermes (related to Mercury), represents the evolution of consciousness and form of the present humanity—the level of the average man with his intellect just rising above the level of earth's horizon.

The sphinx represents the real Self, which has the answers to the riddle of existence and the universe. A woman's head with lion's body shows perfect blend of male and female forces. This is the state of one who has finished his necessary rounds of incarnation and has "broken the Wheel" of Karma. The blue color of the sphinx relates it to the Cosmic Memory—the stored-up knowledge of Cosmic processes derived from the Sphere of Mercy on the Tree of Life.

Involution and evolution are occurring simultaneously as the wheel turns. It teaches that every happening is the result of causes which preceded it. It has also been said that the whirling or rotary motion is the only one which sustains a self-supported body. The same law of motion applies to planets and to atoms, both of which revolve around a center, and include polarities, or duality within Unity.

Jewels of the Wise

The rim of the wheel is a line without beginning or end, like a circle, eternity, incessant equilibrium.

Ezekiel's wheels of life in the Bible, Ezekiel I, were called "wheels within wheels," having rims and spokes, and the rims were filled with eyes, or consciousness. Each was attached through spirit to a four-winged, four-faced living creature whose four faces are those represented in Key 10 and again in Key 21.

"Each creature had the figure of a man, and the face in front was that of a man, at the back that of an eagle, on the right side the face of a lion, and on the left, the face of an ox." All this took place at the level of earth below the heavenly realm. In Revelation 4, similar creatures again appear, but before a throne in heaven.

The clouds are reminiscent of those in which Jesus was taken up when he ascended to heaven, and these reappear again in Key 21. He said he would return in the same way. Clouds are used here to veil the secret nature of the Inner Worlds. They also refer to Jupiter, hurler of thunderbolts and storm.

This Key represents the direction West, which is ahead of us where day ends and the workman receives his pay, both material and spiritual, and harvests his crop according to the seeds which he selected to plant at the beginning of day in the East, represented by Key 3.

If the average man could become less concerned with measuring wealth in material goods, he would find more gain on all levels, especially the kind he could take with him.

The Wheel of Fortune: Key 10

Path 22
The Faithful Intelligence

Equilibration *Sign Libra*

Key 11

JUSTICE

Letter L   **Lamed – Ox-Goad**

Love not in word or speech, but in Deed and in Truth.
(1 John 3:18)

Whereas Key 10 showed a grasp of Universal Law, Key 11 shows the application of the same Law. The ornament on the front of her crown also refers to the accomplishment of the previous lesson—the circle within the square showing activity (red) of the Spirit manifesting outward into form—but here their usual colors are reversed to signify the blending of polarities in this Key.

The subconscious aspects of being have now developed into balanced maturity, able to take the seat of authority and go to work. As the polar opposite of Key 4 The Emperor, Justice represents the opposite sign of the zodiac—he is Aries and she is Libra.

She still retains the underlying properties of The High Priestess, shown by the blue undergarment of the subconscious memory stream, along with the green cape of The Empress, Venus, who is also ruler of Libra. She has not relinquished this color of growth, beauty and charm, even in action, but retains the feminine assets to use as a secondary tool.

The touches of white garb held over from Key 8 Strength now shine through in one shoe as spiritual understanding, and the yoke of her gown shows two quarters of a circle defined by a "T." She is the half-way point (half-circle) between The Magician and The Cosmos, Keys 1 and 21.

Within the yoke, the indigo T represents *Tav*, or Saturn, the planet which is exalted in Libra and here unites its influence with Venus to help bring about the limitation of divine substance into form. The achievement of control through discipline assures the beauty of these forms, as any skilled artisan creates beauty only if his fingers and mind are well-trained and disciplined, this being a work of Saturn.

As Empress of Key 3 she was also a ruler, but only of the inner realm, as she waited quietly in order to foster growth. Here the growing "green" of Venus has matured to a fruitful red, not only its opposite color, but also the color symbolizing the square of manifestation.

Having developed to the point of ruling herself, she may now rule others. Having overcome partiality and bias, the former black-and-white pillars have blended into gray, along with the pomegranates now risen to the top. She is at last able to judge others without favoritism; and only one who has achieved such impartiality as to judge with impersonal detachment, tempered with Mercy as symbolized by her blue sleeves, has the right to judge at all.

Her compassion is not an outer thing worn for show; it is worn within, having become a basic garment, as an essence or foundation over which the cloak of action-red is draped.

This outer robe is of the color of Mars, ruler of her opposite and balancing sign Aries, he having bestowed it upon her as a token of their equality, as she has learned to act more positively and less emotionally.

The blending male and female forces have brought about a balance within herself, and in this balance, she is able to weigh other things which are imperfect and to justly regulate them, her decisions aimed at bringing things back into balance.

This balance is brought about by equalizing opposite forces or polarities, as shown by the gray theme of throne and floor.

Justice: Key 11

The pans of the scales are like two halves of a sphere which, put together, would make a whole. Justice must be measured out with fairness until each pan holds an equal weight and they rest evenly.

The scales, like the hilt of the sword, are of the golden metal ascribed to the Sun—solar energy being present in this work. Gold also edges the crown, its triple ornament suggesting by its shape the Hebrew letter *Shin* of Key 20 Judgment. Shin represents the spiritual fire which releases human consciousness from limitation of ordinary three-dimensional sense-experience.

In many versions of the Tarot, Keys 8 and 11 are reversed in sequence, but this is hardly logical, due to the fact that Libra does not precede Leo in the Zodiac. All the other signs are in their correct chronological order.

The number 11 admirably fits this Key. It is made up of two 'ones" standing equally side by side. This is the middle of the Tarot series, the Key upon which all others pivot when they are lined up in rows of seven with the zero Key above them all. The two "ones" suggest equilibrium, poise, and balance, as does the sign Libra, to which the Key refers.

Libra is the middle sign of the zodiac, or that which begins the second half of the wheel—the "distaff" side (as the marital partner), Aries having begun the first half. The two balance pans could be said to refer to the two halves of the zodiac wheel and the two polarities. Justice is often depicted wearing a blindfold in exact contrast to the opposite Key 4, whose function is Sight.

We might add here that Eve has now become a "helpmeet for Adam." She has experienced the sunlight of Reality, shown behind her as radiant Light. But the drapes are heavy and must be actively tied back to reveal the Light.

These drapes refer to the cycles and mechanical aspects of all manifestation, Jupiter's influence shown by the royal purple.

Such observable factors seem to veil the Living Reality behind them, when one becomes involved in studying the intricacies of ever-turning "wheels within wheels." It is interesting to note that the veil of Cosmos in Key 21 is also a violet colored letter relating to Jupiter, those things which are exoteric concealing the full revelation.

The Hebrew letter of this Key is *Lamed*, which means, as a noun, primarily "ox-goad"—the goad of action which nips the heels of Aleph, the Cosmic Ox of Life-Breath. The letter is shaped like a serpent now opened up and active. Here the hidden magnetic forces go into full action.

One of the activities of this force is to drive one *up* the ladder of spirituality as though a dragon were breathing at your heels. For God is both the Divine Breath and the Directive Power which stirs it up— the *pinata* and the stick which breaks it.

Lamed also means, as a verb, "to teach" or instruct. Instruction itself becomes a goad to right action, inciting the student to keep on, guiding him through "the long circuit of existence." Remember the words of the Lord to Paul in Acts 26: 14: "Saul, Saul, why do you persecute me? It hurts to kick against the goads." Paul had been zealously persecuting Christians, kicking against the very prods which sought to move him in another direction.

The Teacher of Key 5 is also the Ox of Taurus, and the ox goad helps stir up inner instruction. True education is not the accumulation of facts, of theories, or of degrees. It has the purpose of bringing one back through experience into contact with the true Source of all wisdom, as well as to train man in how to act constructively and to make use of the tools God has given him.

Action, Work, and Karma are the functions of this Key; for the literal meaning of the Sanskrit word *Karma* is "deed," implying work or action. Karma is the Law of Cause and Effect, of action and consequence.

Jesus said He came not to destroy the Law, but to fulfill it; and "As ye sow, so shall ye also reap." Karma is not fate, but simply a matter of sowing and reaping—a continuous process with both occurring simultaneously. This truth is so simple that most Bible students miss it.

The memory patterns of subconscious activity work through Karma, for we are judged by our own acts and words, recorded in the memory of Nature and of our own Soul. We can change our harvest any time by changing the seeds or deeds we plant.

Remember the words of the *Book of Activity*: "Your action shall be your prayer." Since there is no such thing as inaction, the fruit of so-called "inactivity" is simply loss of faculty—atrophy.

"When the scales are balanced in reaping effects, there is no vindictiveness; it is the working of the Law. Because the Law is in His consciousness, and it automatically happens," says our Teacher.

The hilt of the sword shows the T-cross of Saturn. The sword of Zain and of discrimination, which divided the male and female in Key 6, is now ready to help reunite them; for the woman has achieved the Truth of right discernment, or choice, which is not prejudiced. Mentally, one uses the sword of discrimination to eliminate everything useless in life, such as outworn memories and attachments and all negative thought, action or emotion.

Elizabeth Browning said, in *A Drama of Exile*, "The sword's hilt is the sharpest, and cuts through the hand that wields it."

A sword refers both to the power of the Word and to the aggressive action of the Mars energy fashioned of his metal, steel. But this metal is tempered with love, and it is given only to those who have risen above the temptation to use it impulsively.

The sword is also a symbol of the element Air, in reference to the tools on The Magician's workbench. A sword helps eliminate mistaken thought or action and cuts out the errors of past consequences as one would separate weeds from grain to give the latter a chance to grow better.

As The Magician lifted his wand for the Will of God to flow through, Justice holds up her sword that her Word and decision be divinely directed. The sword which King Arthur pulled from the anvil has been likened to the Sword of Spirit pulled forth from baser metal.

As the twenty-second Path on the Tree of Life, Lamed is called The Faithful Intelligence. Faith is the substance of things hoped for. We might say the answers to our prayers are molded out of Faith. True Faith becomes a habitual conviction that all things work together for good to those who love God and "whose imagination is stayed on Him."

The Hebrew word for "faithful" is *Amn*, equivalent to our word Amen—the word whereby a prayer is confirmed. Other meanings of the Hebrew *Amn* are "verily" or "truly", and "so be it."

It is likely that when Jesus pronounced this word, it sounded like "Ameen," for present day Assyrians, who still use the Aramaic language of Jesus, speak it thus.

PYTHAGOREAN TRIANGLE

The 47th Theorem of Pythagoras: "In a right-angled triangle the square described on the hypotenuse is equal to the sum of the squares described on the other two sides. "

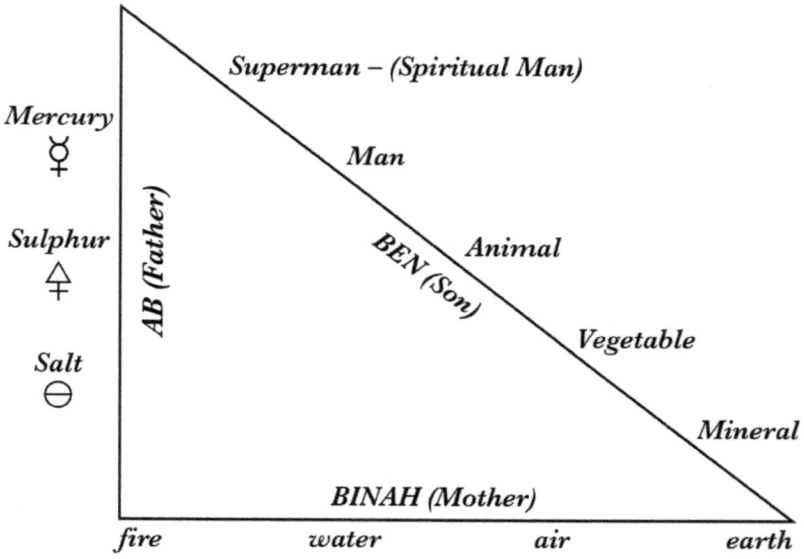

Justice: Key 11

Path 23
The Stable Intelligence

Reversal *Planet Neptune*

Key 12

SUSPENDED MAN

Letter M   **Mem – Waters**

He hath founded the earth upon the Seas, and established it upon the floods.
(Psalm 24)

Mem, the Hebrew letter assigned to this Key, means "seas" or "waters," being the equivalent of our English letter M. In both alphabets, it is the thirteenth letter, but in Greek, as the twelfth letter, it is called *Mu*.

This picture does not represent a physical body as such, nor does it indicate pain or punishment, but rather, suspension of conscious activity, a reversal of consciousness and a sort of mystical isolation, and withdrawal from the world of sense and form.

The wise man realizes that his life does not depend upon material things, neither on people, places or possessions, but that his sole support is the Ultimate Reality of that Above—the invisible realm of Spirit where lies the First Cause at the heart of all things.

While God is not necessarily up by physical direction, He is there, just as He is within; and the first concept of God and of spiritual elevation was thought of as above. Truly He does dwell above the level whereon humanity dwells—not in place, but in upliftment and consciousness. Until one learns to find God within himself and all things or beings, he can only look up.

So, his first deliberate act in changing from the old man to the new is to literally up-end his consciousness from the old way. He must drastically change his ways of thinking and acting until the Truth becomes ingrained within him. He must give up thinking of the earth as his support and walk on the floors of heaven. Until he gets there in consciousness, he can only reach it from below. Once there, he can again right himself as the Dancer of Key 21, who has overcome limitation and attained to a higher state.

The Path of Mem on the Tree of Life is called the Path of Stable Intelligence. The stability comes with removing our feet from a terrestrial platform and placing them solidly on the foundation of Spiritual Reality, then letting God take care of the rest. "Seek ye first the Kingdom of Heaven and all these things shall be added unto you." (Matthew 6:33)

When we really give up, we depend on Him alone Who is both our Source and Destination. The only bond of contact is shown here as the white rope which holds one suspended above the earth. The twisted cord symbolizes the spiraling Force of the radiant White Light of Spirit.

A quotation from Zen teachings: "The branches of a tree are shaken by the storm; but the trunk remains unmoved. In like manner, as the Mind of the arhat is bound to the firm pillar of samadhi by the cord of the four paths, it remains unmoved—even when the body is suffering pain."

The gallows somewhat suggest pillars, but are shaped like the letter *Tav*, the final letter of the Hebrew alphabet, which symbolizes complete attainment. Thus, he has chosen to limit himself within whatever restrictions of discipline may be needed to accomplish this attainment. He has voluntarily bound himself to his goal.

The trees are of living wood—rooted in the ground. The branches have been lopped off, six on either side, to denote trimming away the surface appearance of personality to get down to basics (the twelve

Suspended Man: Key 12

personalities resulting from the twelve signs of the zodiac are only superficial differences).

The earth has been hollowed out beneath his head to make room for the Illumination to take place. Some of the "world" has been given up. With the mental processes taking place below ground, or below the level of consciousness; this depicts a subconscious process. The green growth, the work of imagination, is shown at either side.

His head is placed at the same level as the tree roots to show that basic growth patterns are being changed at the Source, and new Light forming at the very life-roots of his being. His earthly foundation is being spiritualized.

This could not happen until the old sediment had been released from heart and mind; but once the Light is turned on, all darkness must flee henceforth as when Light is turned on in a room.

In such a reversed pattern, all the sediment of former ways would sink to the head in this lowly position. The battle with darkness here would be a mental one, and his cleansing is of the mind, both conscious and subconscious.

Having given up former pathways, his yellow-shod feet are turned upwards toward the Sun; yellow indicating that the Path of Intellect has carried him here.

The previous Key 11 Justice, took him through a process where debts were paid, where the scales were evened up and the Books of Life balanced. He need not wait for life to knock the props out from under him before he accepts that there is no other Way than the Divine One. He is learning to accept the only true Support so that he will not be at the mercy of circumstance. The heavenly Support cannot be taken from any man.

In turning from the old ways, whether within or without, there is a complete reversal of thought and habit patterns, which must be set with care and deliberation. These may seem unnatural at first, even to the individual, but the ways of the Wise always look upside-down to the flesh-blinded eyes of the material-minded.

One is at first conscious of this reversal as though looking at his own reflection in a pool of water where he can see himself mirrored in an upside-down position. This, again, is a prevision of Key 21, The World, whose final perfection is now seen "as in a glass darkly," the number 12 itself being a reversal of the number 21.

A person in this position would find his pockets emptied out of all memories, trends, and thoughts of yore. He would both literally and figuratively straighten out his affairs, clear up any loose ends and tell old comrades "good-bye," as though preparing his last Will and Testament—which he is—by giving up his personal will to the Will of God.

Like Moses, he then walks out into the "sea," where the waters of consciousness part to let him pass, and again close in behind him, while the weapons of "this world" hurled after him avail naught. In another age Jesus, too, entered the waters of Jordan and took up His mission from which there was no turning back. Purification is suggested in this Key by the inversion of things natural or earthly.

The letter of this Key, *Mem*, means "water," and is called one of the three Mother letters of the Hebrew alphabet, referring to the three elements which combine to constitute Earth. These three are *Mem* (water), *Aleph* (air), and *Shin* (fire). The result is shown by *Tav* (earth) perfected, and the Great Work of Alchemy completed.

Water, on the esoteric level, refers to the stream of consciousness, the ever-flowing "mind-stuff." Yoga teaches that "when the lake of mind-stuff is perfectly clear, it mirrors the Light of the Spiritual Sun."

When this continual vibrational flow is restrained, through coming under intelligent direction, it becomes quiet and intense. This ocean of subconscious mentality reflects the personal existence. It is called "water" because it resembles that element with its flowing currents, moving and swirling.

This Astral Fluid is composed of the droplets of energy which are the primary substance of all things and which take form through the activity of Mind. When all of the droplets are culminated together in one place and the earth becomes flooded, a Baraka, or Ship of Wisdom, must be built to carry man back across the waters to God, His Source.

In a sense, this Key also represents the Deluge as in the time of Noah, when all the old evils and impurities of the world were washed away by floods of water that man might begin anew with only the choicest of all things saved out as "seed" for the new. The spiritualized being places in the ark (the Baraka) of his own bodily temple just the essence of all that was good of himself, and lets the rest wash away unresisting.

Neptune, the significator of this Key, verifies its association with water. He was called ruler of the deep, or mystic god of the sea. As a planet, it is related to mysticism as well as to sleep and silence.

Neptune, ruling the Deep of the collective subconscious, is also ruler of Pisces, sign of the fishes, and twelfth sign of the zodiac where unto all the others have poured their influences.

The stillness of Samadhi is not that of idleness. One in motionless meditation may be participating in vital work. In such a state, darkness is extinguished by Light as one goes beyond thought to vision and direct perception.

This experience is Neptunian in nature. Once having direct spiritual experience, one finds it difficult to return to any former pattern of living while knowing that there is more. His former concepts are now reversed to the opposite of those manifested by ordinary mortals.

Jesus taught in the Piscean Age. His first disciples were fishermen. He had twelve Apostles, who are also called in the Book of Revelations the Twelve Foundations upon which rest the Holy City, or New Jerusalem.

The number 12 combines 1 with 2—positive with negative, even as the net of the fisherman is composed of crisscross lines, or positive intersecting negative.

Twelve is the total number of lines of any cube and has been called "the most solid number," being the "foundation of our spiritual and temporal happiness." It is the number of divisions of the heavens into signs of the zodiac and of the twelve tribes which are called "Gates of the City."

The shape of the Suspended Man suggests a 4 placed above a 3 (the legs above the triangular position of the arms). Three times four equals twelve—the number of this Key.

The red color suggests energetic activity which has here been stilled from running. The four also refers to Key 4 and Reason. The logic which once supported and carried him along has temporarily been restrained—the worldly logic of The Emperor reversed. Red color refers to fire, blue to water.

The suggestion of Peter would appear to indicate that the church, being the body of Christ, is shown as negative, receptive, to the positive aspect of Christ, or Spirit.

The buttons and jacket edging are of the lunar metal silver, with water–affinity. The silver cross shows crucifixion of the negative elements within the being. Ten buttons refer to the ten spheres on the Tree of Life.

A student under spiritual training and discipline can hope for no Illumination until the old dross is drained out and washed away. The less he resists, the faster it happens. Underneath all this, a Light begins to grow.

The white hair indicates an "old soul," though in a young body. This One is ready for the final spiritual work, having passed through many lifetimes and having become an "Ancient of Days." He is old and young at the same time; the Absolute Cosmic Consciousness being reflected into the area of personal awareness.

Suspended Man: Key 12

Path 24
The Imaginative Intelligence

Transformation *Sign Scorpio*

Key 13

TRANSITION
(Formerly called Death)

Letter N   **Nun – Fish**

Be faithful unto death, and I will give you the crown of Life.
(Revelation 2:10)

The Hebrew letter *Nun*, when used as a noun, means "fish," but as a verb, it indicates "to sprout" or "to grow." Fishes are symbolic, both of prolific growth and reproductive power.

The glyph of a fish was used by early Christians, who drew one in the sand with a stick to identify themselves when encountering strangers whom they thought to be fellow travelers, in days when Christianity was forced to go underground for preservation.

The natural habitat of fish is water—the element just discussed in the previous Key 12 of Mem. So *Nun* represents the essence of life which is drawn from the waters—the first creatures of conscious life which had the capacity for motion.

The fish has many symbolic meanings, among which are the progress of the world across the primordial waters of unformed realities, or of worlds dissolved and not as yet refashioned.

The function of this Key is called Locomotion and Change. It depicts physical change being achieved through motion.

The fish must be raised out of the water in order to make use of its powers. In alchemical symbolism, as in life, this can only be done with the use of a fishhook. In the Hebrew alphabet, the letter *Tzaddi*

Jewels of the Wise

of Key 17 means "fishhook." Its function is meditation, and logically, meditation is the tool used to catch the spiritual powers symbolized by the mysterious Fish.

This brings about subtle changes within the person by raising up the power of the self-destroying scorpion through the life-and-death stages of the serpent-power of male energy. It progresses on up to the exaltation of the eagle with fully liberated power. All of these things are emblems of Scorpio.

The sign correlating with this Key of Nun is the water sign Scorpio, which is described as relating to death or transition, inheritance, sex, occult practice and regeneration.

All of these things, if you consider them closely, take man "one step beyond" the norm—carrying life forward into a different realm. There is no turning back once you have crossed fully into a state of change or transformation.

It is somewhat like opening a door into another world, or passing through a dark tunnel towards an open end. The door looks mysterious, even fearful, from the earthly side. This is only true because you have never seen past it; the fear of death is mainly fear of the unknown.

Transition is basically change, the act or state of passing from one place, condition or action to another, transformation from one state to another. All matter changes, its material components being liberated into the elements to recombine in other forms. Nothing is ever lost. The Soul-essence does not change except as it evolves, but is liberated from its encasement in a physical shell in order to permit experience of life on higher planes and to digest what was learned here—to rest before again returning in another form.

The symbols of this Key point to a place between the visible and invisible realms, making it like a passageway through which influences act and react between the two worlds. Occultism is a study of the unknown, the inner wisdom which is revealed only to those who open that secret door and pass within.

Regeneration is a state of transformation, the spiritual generation which brings about liberation from death through giving life-consciousness to the eternal, spiritual vehicle.

Scorpio is a fixed water sign ruled by Pluto, Lord of the Underworld, and co-ruled by Mars, the fiery god of action. The Mars force is activated in Scorpio, and the red background here implicates both Mars and the element of fire, which it brings to bear.

After the flood, which covered the earth in Noah's time, had washed away the world's iniquity and impurities, the sun shone hotly to evaporate the waters and dry the land, and the ark landed. Here we see what was left following the destruction of the "world" by water in symbolic form, but relating to the development of an individual. After the flood, only a "skeleton crew" remained—Noah and his family, and pairs of creatures for a nucleus from which to reseed and replenish the earth.

In an old Egyptian myth, there was said to be an inert waste of waters called *Nun*, and these waters were stirred to activity by the movement of Amun, god of wind and air (or spirit) over it. This sounds like the Biblical story of creation, or re-creation.

The desire nature has been purified by these drastic experiences, as shown by the white rose (also an emblem of Uranus which is exalted in Scorpio). The Fool passed through this same level of vibration on his way back into incarnation before re-entering the earthly atmosphere, and here plucked his white rose.

The placement of this Key on the Tree of Life between *Netzach*, Victory, and *Tiphareth*, Beauty (or the Sun), indicates this stage as the spiritualization of the desire nature with the Christ-force flowing through.

When the reversal of consciousness begun in the previous Key has fully taken place, one literally *dies* to the old life, and for a while is like unleavened bread—all the earthly flesh (symbolically) dissolved from his bones. Let us note that yeast leavens bread through a process of fermentation of the dough, causing the production of alcohol and carbon dioxide, also breaking down the organic substances.

The skeleton is completely reversed in the middle portion, being twisted at pelvis and neck so that the backbone is in front. This would be physically impossible, but indicates here a deliberate reversal of the forces of Mars, the so-called "libido" of the psychologist, as well as a change of direction from North to South, or from darkness to Light.

The dynamic Mars force is redirected by this twist of the skeleton, and this fully disintegrates the former false mental structure. The same twist is seen in the river, the stream of consciousness being diverted from its original direction and turned toward the Sun.

The rising sun in the eastern background refers to *Tiphareth*, the sixth sphere on the Tree of Life. What outwardly appears as death is but moving into the sunrise of a new day; when yesterday passes, tomorrow is born. Yet he is walking more nearly southward, away from the dark of ignorance and the unknown, toward the dawn of higher consciousness and enlightenment.

Just as the skeleton is the basis and framework of the body, essential to all physical motion, so Transition has been called "the framework of existence." Evolution can only occur if there is change, with elimination of the outworn.

To hold onto outmoded things and ways of life is to cause impaction and constipation of life and affairs. In biology, Scorpio also refers to the area of elimination. Good health depends upon this function. This does not mean willful disruption of lives and affairs, but letting go of that which has really passed its usefulness.

When you walk over the desolation caused by the outgrown and decaying past, mourn it not. You have garnered already your seed for another sowing, and the chaff can either fertilize next year's field or serve to fire a furnace.

> *"His winnowing fork is in His Hand, and He will clear His threshing floor, and gather His wheat into the granary; but the chaff He will burn with unquenchable fire."* (Matthew 3:12)

Chaff is but the outer covering of the grain, and has finished its mission when the grain is gathered. Remember that within yourself you carry the seed of your own future. It is the living nucleus which gives you authority over a new life after the ash of the past is gone. It is the Holy of Holies, and you do "take it with you" through all movement and change—even through transition.

"He who loseth his life shall find it." (Matthew 16:25) We must let go. The miracles of transformation depend upon this.

Putrefaction is the actual alchemical stage which correlates with this Key. An old alchemical treatise stated: "Unless your matter putrefies, it may in no wise be truly altered, nor may your elements be divided kindly."

In Key 13 the seed is depicted by the double oval in the upper left corner. This is a symbol showing the process of manifestation. The five rays extending from the inner oval represent the four elements, fire, air, earth, and water, plus the fifth essence called "ether," or akasha.

The seed of Scorpio is the cell separated from the parent body while containing within itself all of the inherent parental characteristics.

The scythe is a tool traditionally carried by the grim reaper. It is shown with a blade of steel, the metal of Mars, with a T-shaped handle suggesting *Tav*, the letter of Saturn and of the end of Time.

Transition marks the time of harvesting the fruits of life. In the autumn of the year, when frost comes to lay waste the fields, a farmer goes out to cut down what remains of his crop. He harvests the fruits, and saves out from them the very best of the seed to plant for the coming year. Thus release of the plant is not the end of life itself.

Consciousness is not destroyed. Neither does the consciousness of any person die. It merely moves on to another environment, relieved of its heavy earth-vehicle. It is free, and can later choose a new vehicle as one would choose an automobile.

The earth in this Key looks black, referring to the vast Unknown, or the return of vegetation to its state of primal Matter. It appears that new seedlings are already sprouting and taking root in the fertile ground for next year's crop in the black silt remaining after the flood water has left its rich sediment and is drained away.

The heads of the king and queen represent the Supernals, Wisdom and Understanding, the Abstract male and female Principles of Creation on the Tree of Life. The wheel replaces hands of older version to show progress possible in new activities.

The emptied boot shows an empty shell as all that remains of the passing Piscean age. Pisces physically rules the feet.

The number 13 has long been called unlucky. This is usually said to be because of Jesus and the twelve apostles. But more basically in the science of numbers, 12 is a complete rounded number—3 times 4—but to go beyond is to wander into strange realms. To one who cannot see beyond the physical, death appears as a fearful enemy.

Read all of I Corinthians 15. St. Paul gives a description of transition and resurrection. He said: "We shall not all die, but we shall all be *changed*..." We must change our own thinking to change our lives.

The Path of this Key is called The Imaginative Intelligence. By changing one's basic ideas, he forms new patterns of life and the old ones "die." Right use of the imaginative faculties will set in motion the subtle action which impels from within the upward rather than downward movement of the Mars force.

Life is a continuous process of change, or transformation from lower to higher stages of being and manifestation. Behind the outer mask of death is taking place the whole ascent of life in Spirit.

Sometimes the bones in this Key are colored pink to denote livingness. Remember, the reference here is not to bodily death, nor physical destruction. The "secret" is shown only to the pure in heart. Outer death cannot compare with the mystical death which takes place while the body still lives, and which consists in a total change of consciousness from that of mortality to immortality. This is a very real (but not a common) thing which happens to those on the Divine Path.

Jesus is the Greek form of the Hebrew name Joshua, *Shua* meaning "to be freed," and Joshua, or *Y'shua*, meaning "salvation, aid, deliverance." Joshua was the son of *Nun*, "the fish," the letter of this Key. Then "Liberation, the Son of Fish," suggests that the power of Truth, which frees the individual, correlates with coming down to the bare basics of Creation—the growth-to-come implied.

As Mem represents waters, *Nun* represents the life beneath those waters which we seek to draw out in order that we may partake of the fruits of spirit.

Path 25
The Intelligence of Probation

Verification   *Sign Sagittarius*

Key 14

TEMPERANCE

Letter S **Samekh – Tent-Peg**

Then I saw another mighty angel coming down from heaven, wrapped in a cloud, with a rainbow over his head, and his face was like the sun, and his legs like pillars of fire.... And the angel whom I saw standing on sea and land lifted up his right hand to heaven and swore by Him who lives forever and ever, who created heaven and what is in it...that in the days of the trumpet call to be sounded by the seventh angel, the mystery of God as He announced to His servants, the prophets should be fulfilled. (Revelation 10:1)

The Hebrew letter for Key 14 is *Samekh*. It is shaped like a serpent swallowing its tail. In other words, it represents completion of the work of controlling the fiery "serpent" forces within us and their transformation into higher occult powers.

This work began in Key 8 Strength, when the letter *Teth* was drawn as a coiled serpent, as yet inactive. In Key 11 Justice the letter *Lamed* clearly depicts the same serpent force uncoiled in action. Now he has reversed his first position to close the circle and complete the course.

The Magician, or mind-personality, can now lay down his girdle; for with this Key, man's personal efforts have taken him as far as he can go unaided. The time has come for higher forces to step down and take a hand in placing him on the spiritual Path.

The heavenly hierarchy is represented here by the Archangel Michael of the Sun. Michael literally means "one who is like God." His white gown represents purity, and the Hebrew letters IHVH just below the neckline show whence he came, exactly like the white undergarment of The Fool.

> *"And there was war in heaven: Michael and his angels fought against the dragon...and the great dragon was cast out, that old serpent called the devil..."* (Revelation 12:7)

Michael, whose habitat is the fiery Sun, performs his work of casting out Satan by trying each spiritual aspirant in the fiery furnace in order to burn out all dross and impurities and refine the gold within him, so that he may be proven worthy to be called a Son of God.

This is the beginning of the "Great Work of the Sun," spoken of by alchemists; and Michael, His agent, comes to prepare the temple to make it ready and fit for the Most High when He comes.

The lion is colored red to represent the alchemical Sulphur, or Fire. This quality within the individual is being modified by the astral fluid flowing from the vase, which represents the stream of subconscious activities.

The first destruction of godlessness in the world, and the cleansing thereof, was by floods of water in the time of Noah, as told:

> *" 'And I will establish my covenant with you; never again shall all flesh be cut off by the waters of a flood, and never again shall there be a flood to destroy the earth.' And God said to Noah, 'This is a sign of the covenant which I make between me and you and every living creature that is with you, for all future generations: I set my bow in the cloud, and it shall be a sign of the covenant between me and the earth...the waters shall never again become a flood to destroy all flesh.' "* (Genesis 9:11-15)

But God said the next time He destroyed the world, it would be done by fire. The Sun represents the Fire element. Fire is also the symbol of Spirit.

The whole keynote of this card is the contrast of fire and water. Fire and water are most unlike elements, and when brought together, they react violently to "put each other out," or combine forces to produce steam, a source of great power. This is a secret of the use of opposing forces in our lives—not to react against, but to seek a way to use these forces for general good. After the flood, the sun came out and dried up the water.

The rainbow is caused by the sun shining through mist, made up of water droplets in the atmosphere. It causes the refraction of the Sun's pure white or colorless light into its seven component parts, the colors of the solar spectrum.

The seven-pointed star also shows seven rays of golden Light, or seven phases of the One Force, the Seven Spirits of God. This star requires a special skill to draw geometrically correct and is, therefore, a symbol of mastery.

A rainbow is somewhat like a smile breaking through tears, much as sunshine overcomes a shower. This, too, is a form of mastery.

The mythological goddess of the rainbow was called Iris. She and Mercury were both messengers, and were called on at different times to serve the gods. Iris wore a cloak of many colors, her shining garments trailing across the sky in a rainbow curve. The Rider version of Temperance refers to the goddess by showing Iris flowers growing at the angel's feet.

There is a real pot of gold at the end of this rainbow! That is the gold of spiritual attainment and the perfected being. For the true work of alchemy is to refine the gold within the individual—the gold called Sol, or Sun. The Golden Force streaming from the Great Sun is shown in the background of this Key.

Spiritual riches have been discovered and the human quest is ended. But the work of Spirit is about to increase as man turns himself over to the Higher Powers to continue his evolvement.

The Hebrew name for Sagittarius is *Qeseth*, and the same word is used for "bow," so the sign Sagittarius fits very well for this Key to which it has been attributed.

Sagittarius is a fire sign. Its symbol is drawn like a bow and arrow. The arrow representing directed Will is sent forth to pierce the rainbow, and to raise the consciousness. The higher the aim, the higher the goal. The fiery forces within man must be rightly directed in order to lift him to higher accomplishment.

As the result of this released force, a certain vibratory motion is set up. The dictionary defines vibration as "motion back and forth," or to quiver, or shake. Our atmosphere is filled with this invisible motion, or energy. We live in a vibratory universe, and the same laws at work on the earth plane also bring us the radiant energy from the Sun.

This Key is called Temperance because through the process of fire on water, and water on fire, our own "metal" is being tempered, and our "mettle" tried. It has to do with bringing together exact opposites in order to modify both through interaction.

As an alchemist wrote: "Fire and flowing water are contrary to one another, happy art thou if thou canst unite them. Let it suffice thee to know this."

The Qabalistic Path of this Key is called the Path of Tentative Intelligence, and of Probation or Trial, situated on the Tree of Life as the channel between Tiphareth and Yesod.

Probation here is meant in the sense of proving, through testing and tempering. It means verification, the application of what you have learned put into actual practice so you can see how much of it is true and how much you have actually mastered.

It is said: "Truth is established by trial." We must step out on what we have learned. Just learning the theory is not enough unless we can prove it in actual practice.

Temperance: Key 14

Tempering imparts strength to the object being treated. The use of opposing forces brings about equilibration as a result. Our mental patterns can also be changed by bringing into play an opposite condition.

This Path has been called "the first test whereby the Creator tries the Compassionate," that is, those advanced beings slated to become Compassionate Brothers unto those below them in the evolutionary scale.

The white eagle represents the water sign Scorpio in a regenerated condition of purity. Flames of fire are being dropped on his head in the form of five yods from a torch in the angel's hand. Here the yods represent the fiery Life Power as it breaks up into the five modes of manifestation—fire, air, earth, and water, plus their composite element, ether. The lion and eagle also depict the animal nature, or Vital Soul, which is being worked upon from above.

The angel dips one foot into the psychic or subconscious world, and his head in the Sun. It is here that human consciousness rises from the level of the astral plane to the consciousness of the Son, and his experiences at this stage may quite possibly include some from the psychic world.

The other foot rests upon the earth, the realm of physical form. Transformation must occur on both the conscious and subconscious levels in order to accomplish the spiritual work.

Michael holds the "vase of art," the vessel of the Soul, that furnace which is the body; and from this the waters of consciousness pour forth. To this must be applied the fire of Spirit in order to transmute the gold. He has "taken in hand" the human personality, in order to raise it.

Michael is called the Holy Guardian Angel, symbol of the Divine Presence forever overshadowing us, always available at our call for guidance and help. One must invite the contact by confidently expecting it and lifting the consciousness toward its level.

The number 14 reduces to 5, number of The Teacher. There is a correlation between the two in the sense that both have to do with the inner guidance of the individual. If the inner hearing depicted in Key 5 is well-developed, the Guardian Angel will have an easier time getting through.

His wings are red to show the fiery aspect of the sign Sagittarius, and the highlights are of the blue color attributed to that sign. The path behind him is the Path of Return, shown also in Key 18 The Moon. It rises in wave-vibration pattern to a point between the twin peaks which represent Chokmah and Binah, or Wisdom and Understanding.

Hovering above it is the crown of attainment to be inherited by all who "endure to the end," as Jesus said—those who pass the tests and trials without falling by the wayside. The crown is also the Symbol of Kether, the first Sephirah. Rays from the Crown look very much like those from the head of the angel.

The purpose of this Key is to establish the foundation of our house of life as denoted by the letter *Samekh*, which means "tent-peg" or "prop," in the sense of the support of a dwelling—that which firms and stabilizes. The dwelling which interests us now is the Holy Temple or House of God.

Temperance: Key 14

Path 26
The Renewing Intelligence

Mirth *Sign Capricorn*

Key 15

THE DECEIVER
(Formerly called The Devil)

Letter O   Ayin – Eye

Judge not by appearance, for that which appears beareth small resemblance to that which is.

This is *the first of seven steps to spiritual attainment*. It is at this point that you become aware that the Eye of the Lord is in every place, and is upon you minutely in all you do. Because man's own spiritual vision has atrophied from misuse since the Fall of Adam, the beginning of spiritual experience becomes a time of intense awareness of his own lack and need for spiritual sight.

Part of man's lack in spiritual sight is based on his inclination to judge all things by their surface appearance. It is because of this false judgment that man has become bound by chains he forged himself and has become a slave to appearances. In this has been found duality and confusion, yet it is when one reaches the very depth and can see no other way out that he is at last ready for the spiritual Path—to go all the way, having learned the fallacy of other ways.

The Hebrew letter *Ayin* means not only "Eye," but also "fountain" and "outward appearance." Red eyes show the exaltation of Mars, the planet ruling sight, in the earth sign Capricorn, the sign which rules this Key. The Deceiver, this illusion sometimes called the "father of lies," is holding up his palm to full view, trying to tell you that what

Jewels of the Wise

you see before you is all there is—"there isn't any more"—in contrast to The Teacher, who told you that there is always more than is seen or can be revealed.

The contrast of this Key with the previous one underlines the difference between the angel of darkness and the angel of light. It is said in the Qabalah that "with each Soul is sent into the world both a guardian angel and an accusing angel." Key 14 shows the Guardian Angel, who guides us and defends good from evil; but here is shown the accusing one, the opponent or adversary, the enemy of God which is hostile or antagonistic toward that which is good.

He represents that which we create or build up in opposition to what God is. We create our own monstrosity, contrary to all God represents. Therefore it has to be removed so He can come through.

Yet all the attributes wrapped up in this one apparition show the accumulated error of the man and woman who descended (or fell) from Adam and Eve. Man is accused by his own error. Their own mistakes have brought them to this predicament. They have fallen into the mud, and only through the ascent of spirit can they rise like the glistening white lotus out of this situation.

The darkness here is that of fear and ignorance. The dark and "evil" side of life is given power to the extent that we accept or dwell on it. Ignoring it will not always cause it to go away, but one need not accept it as part of his life. The devil never made anyone do anything. Man has the full power of control and direction, and of choice between good and evil.

We have passed through the refiner's fire at the human level with the Archangel Michael on our side to fight for the good. No longer shall we be as ordinary mortals. The outcome of this was to gain control over the occult forces, bringing awareness of the development of certain inner powers made possible through overcoming. But now that very "serpent force," so hardly won, begins to whisper temptations in our ear. He whom we have overcome has decided to use subtlety to gain back his control.

The Deceiver: Key 15

This is the point of choice, where the dread Dweller on the Threshold seeks to prevent our entrance into higher states. Actually, he is testing our worthiness to enter. He asks us to stop right there and not attempt to go any further, by offering us the pleasures of this world. He says: "Why not play with and pervert these powers for the sake of earthly gain." But if the candidate for the Path says, like Jesus: "Get thee behind me, Satan," the battle is won.

The temptation of Jesus in the wilderness was rather in the nature of a postscript. He had already taken the step forward at the baptism, having pleased God and been accepted as His beloved Son. But his readiness to take up the work was still not proven, not brought down to earth. This is where the earthy tempter forced him to show his hand and seal his decision.

The Deceiver is the Dweller on the Threshold who tries to tempt every seeker on The Way to turn into devious other paths than the One Path—all of them seeming easier and pleasanter at the outset, because the grade is downward. But would Jesus be our Lord now if He had chosen the prizes of power and great gain The Deceiver offered Him in the desert?

This Key shows the negative result from over binding in the realm of form. The Path being just beside the Sephirah called Splendor on the Tree of Life makes it possible for them to find their way out through intellectual enlightenment, since wrong use of intellect got them there.

The pentagram, or five-pointed star, is a symbol of man; and placed upside down here it shows man's perversion, the reversal of his true place in the Cosmos, which God promised Adam should be one of dominion.

This first stage of spiritual unfoldment is the point at which one becomes conscious of the world's bondage, and impatient of its hold. The man and woman, or the conscious and subconscious minds, stand in chains loose enough so that as soon as they see their error, and recognize their actual freedom from the domination of darkness, they can remove the chains and walk away.

A hymn to the Egyptian sun god Ra says: "Thy priests go forth at dawn; they wash their hearts with laughter."

The Deceiver presents to our attention a dual world wherein there could be both Good and Evil in direct contradiction to God's Word, after God had made the world and pronounced as "good" everything He had created. The Greek word from which "devil" comes means "slanderer."

> *"And I heard a loud voice saying in heaven, Now is come salvation and strength, and the kingdom of our God, and the power of His Christ: for the accuser of our brethren is cast down which accused them before our God day and night."* (Revelation 12:10)

1 Peter 5:8 says: "Be sober, be vigilant; because your adversary the devil, as a roaring lion, walketh about, seeking whom he may devour: Who resist steadfast in the faith...." The advice of Jesus, however, was "resist not evil, but make way for good." Use the energy constructively to build a good way, rather than spend it fighting the evil.

Capricorn, the sign of this Key, is ruled by Saturn. The Egyptians called this sign Typhon. Its symbol is usually a goat with the tail of a dolphin. Capricorn rules mountains, and is an earth sign, the ruler of the tenth house, the highest in the horoscope—as Capricorn usually rules the heights of worldly ambition, as well as positions of authority.

Yet, it is more than that; for throughout the world, out of the deepest darkness, Capricorn is the sign which witnesses the birth of the avatar. This sign is symbolic of all world redeemers; for the Sun entering Capricorn reaches its lowest point, the shortest day in the year, and will then immediately begin its yearly climb once more to the heights of summer where it will enjoy the longest day. So it is said the Sun is born at the winter solstice, as Light is born out of darkness.

The goat is not a conformist like the sheep. He strays off on independent paths. The dolphin's tail shows that this sign knows the depths, and the goat shows that it also can climb to the heights, thus its influence extends from one to the other.

The Deceiver: Key 15

In the physical body Capricorn rules the knees; and it is when we feel a sense of bondage through muddled affairs that we finally sink to our knees in prayer. Must one wait to be goaded by misfortune into seeking God?

The Path of this Key is called The Renewing Intelligence. When we take stock and recognize how things really stand, we are ready for a program of renewal. Matching wits with the crafty Deceiver helps prepare us by developing skill and judgment.

The feet of this illusionary creature are shown as eagle's claws. These represent misuse of the Scorpio force as does also the smoldering torch. The torch symbolizes the transmission of the Life-force from father to son; but little light is given while it smokes wastefully. It represents basically the misuse of the creative Life Force, diverting it for sense purposes to the generative organs instead of toward regeneration. That is the significance of the tail which man, or conscious mind, has developed—his trademark of membership in the animal kingdom, over which the human Adam had been given rulership.

The female figure, or subconscious mind, has a tail plus a bunch of grapes, as though her fall from grace was caused by tasting forbidden fruit. Since a person is known by his fruits, hers are but of animal nature.

These two are chained to a figure which is only the drawing of a cube, a figure having no dimension, therefore, a false pedestal with a false god seated thereon. Being but the surface of a cube depicts that only surface knowledge of the physical plane is available here.

They are positioned much like the figures in Key 6 The Lovers, but no longer in innocence. Their horns and hooves also show their regression to animal nature. Still, by their intelligent faces, we may assume they will lift their chains when they become sufficiently irked, and face facts.

The bat wings of The Deceiver show him as a night-flying creature. The black background represents the limitation and darkness of ignorance, which also provides a thick veil for hiding the Truth.

The navel shows a Mercury symbol—the upper half of mental-color yellow, and the lower half the red cross of physical activities. The position of the arms is reminiscent of the Magician, but with the feeling reversed through a caricatured benediction.

The function attributed to this Key is Mirth (laughter or merriment), and that is a sure way to dissolve darkness. If we can rise far enough above our troubles to get a good perspective of them, we will see how ridiculous the whole situation appears and how like a comic strip caricature. Then, if we can laugh wholeheartedly at the situation, all seeming devils flee and disappear. Wholesome laughter has a healing, cleansing effect.

The Deceiver: Key 15

Path 27
The Exciting Intelligence

Awakening　　　　　　　　　　　　　　　　　　　*Planet Mars*

Key 16

THE TOWER

Letter P **Peh – Mouth**

As the lightning comes from the East and shines as far as the West, so will the coming of the Son of Man. (Matthew 24:27)

The letter *Peh*, meaning "mouth," is drawn just like the letter *Kaph*, meaning "closed hand," except that a small tongue has been added. It is as though *Peh* gives utterance to that which was comprehended by *Kaph*, the Hebrew letter of Key 10 Wheel of Fortune.

Indeed, it is out of the storm clouds of Key 10 Wheel of Fortune that the lightning-flash of Truth comes forth to destroy all false boundaries and beliefs. The wheels which were set in motion by Kaph may be considered as the winding of a clock; and here in The Tower, the time comes for the alarm to ring—just as you had intended.

From the Wheel of Fortune, in the direction of West and sunset, the pay time of the day, have clouds floated around to the North, the direction of The Tower and the unknown. Here comes a delayed reward out of the darkest hour.

The function of this Key is Spiritual Awakening. But the spiritual flash of Truth which says you must rise now, is not much more appealing at first than the call to get out of bed. When it is still dark and cold outside, the desire is strong to pull the blankets over your head and doze a while longer. In the same way, the new aspirant on the Path has spiritual lapses at first until the Light grows constant and no longer comes in spasmodic flashes.

This Key depicts the second stage of spiritual development, or the stage of waking from the nightmare of delusion depicted by The Deceiver. As long as dreams remain pleasant, man is content to enjoy their illusions, regardless of how fleeting or unfounded they are; and as long as Life serves him up ease and material goods according to his fancy, he finds no reason to seek beyond the level of his body and brain.

But dreams can only last so long, and it is time for him to arise and get busy with his own development and that of his fellows. Then a vicious nightmare may be just the thing needed to startle him awake into reality and to make him glad to rise. He eventually becomes grateful—both for being free of the terror, and for the nightmare itself, which set him free from fanciful delusions.

In the same way, you are reluctantly grateful to the person who strips off the blankets and forces you to rise, to enjoy the sunshine of reality. For your dreams have been unbearable delusions brought about by Adam's fall into the realm of sense, where the devil tried the old "world." What relief to know it was false and that you are free, even though, to the average man, this unreality is all that he believes in.

The "eye" of *Ayin* enabled us to receive visual impressions. Now the "mouth" of *Peh* makes possible our expression of them. While in spiritual darkness, one gathered impressions and founded opinions on things seen in the realms of sense, depicted here by the earthy-brown foundation on which the structure is built, of the same color as The Adversary. But now the tongue is to be tamed—that "unruly member" spoken of in the Book of James, Chapter 3.

The crown being toppled is the false crown of material attainment. Mankind has here come a great way and attained considerable success from an earthly standpoint; but "what profiteth a man if he gain the whole world, and lose his own soul?" The old world must pass away to make room for the new.

The house in this Key was founded upon earthly premises and the attempt was to build from earth to heaven instead of from heaven

The Tower: Key 16

to earth, just as the Tower of Babel attempted to storm heaven's gates by building an earthly structure up to a far-off God instead of preparing the temple of his own vehicle fit to hold the indwelling God already there.

The man here reverses the colors of Key 12 Suspended Man, and exchanges Illumination for the dark locks of ignorance. The woman equally misdirects the purity of Key 2 The High Priestess, and has exchanged the receptive lunar silver of her crown for one of the same shape, but colored only with the yellow aspect of her own thinking.

It seems that after their Fall, they not only clothed themselves to hide their bodies, but separated themselves from their neighbors to the extent that everything appeared as their opponents. That wall of separation is itself a lie and must be brought down so that man can be a brother to his fellow man.

What structures have been built up by the mouth of man! What corruptions of Truth, where false interpretation and the adulteration of personal opinion has been added to the teaching of the ages. And each sect has sought to build a wall about his own beliefs, claiming to hold all of Truth to themselves.

The Path of this Key is called The Exciting Intelligence, whereby is created the spirit of every creature under the Supreme Orb. Mars is called the root of other powers, its exciting influence that which gives the initial impulse to various actions.

Mars, which rules this Key, is a fiery planet, even to the extent of appearing red in the heavens. Its symbolic color is also red. It is a symbol of great energy, of aggression, and both muscular and masculine activity. Its course can be traced through the Tarot Keys beginning from Aries, Mars-ruled, in Key 4 The Emperor, with its function of sight and order.

In Key 13 Transition, Scorpio, co-ruled by Mars, brought about the end of physical manifestation as applied to generation and regeneration.

In Key 15 The Deceiver, Capricorn finds Mars exalted and sight is again exalted, but superficially so. Superficial sight had carried man as far as it could—too far in fact, as in the case of Paul, who overzealously defended the words of the Pharisaic Hebrew law in which he had been educated.

Then came the searing flash of realization which blinded and threw him to earth. And he heard the words of Christ Jesus, through the voice of Spirit, speaking to him from the heavens. In one moment, the structure of centuries was for Paul broken. And he was alone, blind, reversed in belief, not knowing where next to turn.

The couple here, the conscious and subconscious minds, also built up a tower based on the sayings of man, of laws, and letters of the law. There are twenty-two rows of masonry depicted, one for each letter of the Hebrew alphabet; and they have used these both to define and imprison themselves within the narrow strictures of their self-imposed beliefs and tenets which they have considered immutable. These bricks are not composed of the stone of Truth, but of the clay of Adam, dug from the material earth and mixed with the mortar of man's thought.

Outside The Tower are twenty-two flames, representing the spirit of the Word. "For the letter killeth, but the spirit giveth life." (2 Corinthians 3: 6) The words which come through the intellect, the opinions or interpretations of man, are of the letter, but the words which God speaks to or through us are Spirit. They are alive and life-giving.

When these words of Spirit enter our lives, the fire that is in them destroys the outworn cliches by which we have been surrounding ourselves. These are formed like Yods, the creative flame of God, which is the basis of the flame alphabet used to bring forth Truth teachings.

Qabalists believe that the components out of which God formed the world were the ten basic numbers, whereas twenty-two Hebrew letters make up the speech whereby He uttered creation into being—the total called the Thirty-Two Paths of Wisdom.

Seeing correctly must precede speaking correctly because thought and speech are merely superficial until true perception comes. The wagging tongue must be silenced; for, as the Bible says, ' In that day, you shall give account for every idle word you speak." Remember, the Word is creative. God created the world through the Word, and made man in His Image.

The yods at left show a "seeded" figure eight, or a double hexagon. The formation at right is shaped like a Venus symbol, and is also formed in the manner of the ten Sephiroth of the Tree of Life.

By the time of Jesus, the old Mosaic laws had long "laid upon men burdens harder than they could bear," as the authorities added layer upon layer of interpretation, each brick mixed with the clay of their own personalities and opinions.

The lightning Flash here refers to that mentioned in the *Book of Formation*: "The appearance of the ten spheres out of nothing is like a flash of lightning, being without end. His Word is in them when they emanate, and when they return." It is called *Mezla*, or the Holy Influence, which descends from *Kether* to establish the Ten *Sephiroth*. And if you follow its course, it will be seen to zig-zag throughout the Ten Sephiroth in the order they are placed on the Tree of Life.

Lightning, like Mars, is a masculine symbol. It was anciently stated, "The agriculturists call the lightning the fertilizer of the waters, and so regard it."

It proceeds here from a solar disk, showing its source to be the Sun. It also represents the inner occult forces shown by the serpent in Key 10 The Wheel of Fortune, the Cosmic vital electricity. In both Key 6 The Lovers and 10, the serpent is shown on the North side of the picture. Also the dark pillar and sphinx are located on the North side of Key 2 The High Priestess and Key 7 The Chariot.

The fear of the unknown has often caused man to selfishly isolate himself, to nest down into a crystallized structure of false security, thinking if he ignores the darkness, it will go away. The darkness of the unknown indicates that which is outside man's realm of experience; he tried to shut out that which he did not understand.

North is symbolically the place of greatest darkness, since the sun never shines there (in the northern hemisphere). The idea of strength and severity is associated with north, for those powers veiled in darkness, the occult forces, are those which emerge to lead one to liberation and enlightenment.

The lightning which once struck terror to men's hearts has now been harnessed as the great liberating power of electricity, one of the gifts of Aquarius. As stated by the wise men of old, "Out of the North comes splendor."

In older French versions, this Key was called *La Maison Dieu*, or the House of God. It is built on a lonely peak to demonstrate isolation from others. As a vertical cliff or precipice this is distinguished from the promontory, or headland, on which The Fool is standing. The root of the word promontory is *prominere*, "to project," while the root word for "precipice" signifies "climbing up."

Alchemically, the tower represents the athanor, the vessel wherein the work of the alchemist takes place, and where base metals are transmuted to gold.

The Tower: Key 16

Path 28
The Natural Intelligence

Revelation *Sign Aquarius*

Key 17

THE STAR

Letter Tz   **Tzaddi – Fish-Hook**

The Star of meditation leads to the birth of the Christ in you, as the focusing of solar energies transforms the vehicle to receive the Christ Force.

The man and woman shown in Key 16 outside the falling Tower were the two aspects of Mind, the conscious and the subconscious. Now they are shown as twin vessels held in the hands of the Great Mother of Heaven, the original Potter of their clay. Here she is replenishing them with the Waters of Eternal Life. Their orange color is the color of the two Paths of Key 6 The Lovers and Key 19 The Moon.

Having had no choice but to "give up," after the recent rude awakening of Key 16 The Tower, all the hard crystallizations which had been allowed to accumulate in previous times are now to be dissolved and transmuted into the transcendental Elixir of Life. The Great Awakener cannot allow the old encrustations of habit and error to remain, so they are literally washed away.

The symbol for the alchemical process of "dissolution" or dissolving ≈ is the same as the symbol used for the sign and constellation of Aquarius. This should give a clue as to the true nature of the heavenly water being poured by the Water-Bearer. The pouring out of the water refers to distilling of the essences.

The Great Mother here shown is Isis-Urania—Isis, the earth mother goddess; Urania, meaning "the heavenly," a muse of astronomy, and sometimes-goddess. Aquarius rules, among other things, the stars and ethers of space, and is related to this Key 17.

The Truth of Being remains ever-hidden from the profane, and none can remove her veils by force. But to one who has proved his worth and has reached the stage where he can be trusted with the great secrets of Nature and Creation, she reveals herself voluntarily through greater insight into her working.

What man had before thought true now shows itself as the mere folly of the unenlightened masses. But having passed the period of the storm and stress of awakening, a great stillness has come about, as the dawning new day removes the veils of darkness which were its former disguise.

"And behold, the Lord passed by, and a great and strong wind rent the mountains and broke in pieces the rocks..." and after the wind an earthquake, and after the earthquake a fire. But the Lord was in none of these. And after the fire, "a still, small Voice"...the Voice of the Lord in the Silence. (1 Kings 19:11 and 12)

This Path is called The Natural Intelligence, the intelligence which overlays Nature. The beautiful Venus-Urania has long, natural-golden hair, suggestive of the magnetism of solar energies working in earth, and a symbol of natural vitality. She represents that function of the Ego which charges the subconscious with substance and vitality.

The Hebrew letter for this Key is *Tzaddi*, equal to Tz, Ts, or Cz. It means "fishhook," and it is here that the Lord Himself goes to work on us, baiting His Hook and biding His time.

Eventually we take this Hook which the Great Fisherman drops down to us through the waters of the Great Sea of Universal Mind, the realm of the Lord's Subconscious domain, whence He hauls us up to His higher level, ready to make us at One with Him.

The Star: Key 17

Meditation and Revelation are the functions of this Key. We, too, go fishing every time we meditate, waiting till the mind is still, then baiting the hook with a desire to know the answer to what is needed, and awaiting the nibble, the answer from within. Through meditation, the powers of the subconscious are raised to a conscious level, as the fish is lifted out of the pool.

This Key also stands for Truth, so we search in the depths of the Universal Mind-Stuff where all Truth awaits. The hook of meditation is the implement which draws the fish *(Nun)* up from the waters *(Mem)* of suspended mind, where the highest Truths are revealed.

The transforming agent of the Scorpio reproductive power represented by the Fish must be raised up in order to be used as spiritual food. Through meditation we direct solar forces, and transmute energies of nerve-force. The universe itself is built and maintained by thought in the perpetual Self-recognition of the Creator.

One cannot use intellect here, in its superficial sense, but it is the intellect which decides on the quest for Truth, and sets the conditions. Then it moves to the background, becoming still and watchful. The number seventeen is worthy of note here—the one for attention, and the seven for rest.

The red bird depicts an ibis, the fishing bird considered sacred to Hermes, or to Mercury, the god of intellect. His red color indicates an active quest. The scarlet Ibis is known in tropical America, but the revered bird of Egypt was actually black and white. It arrived at that season when the Nile rose each spring, heralding the time of abundance, and left when it receded. It was sometimes called *Abu Hannas*, or "Father John."

The tree on which it rests is shaped to represent the brain and nervous system. The green color of leaves and vegetation indicates the vast amount of growth which takes place during this, the third stage of spiritual unfoldment, helped by the processes of enlargement through imagination.

The Great Sea is another name for the Divine Mother. "God made the firmament ('Heaven'), and separated the waters which were under the firmament from the waters which were above the firmament, and it was so."

The heavenly "waters" are not as earthly waters. Isis-Urania here stands above the level of psychic "waters" of the astral realm, and balances her form by resting one foot upon it. Meditation stabilizes the psychic waters and makes them more "solid." The Truth can only come from areas above the psychic.

When the old consciousness is transformed to bring forth the "new heaven and new earth," she pours the great gift of heavenly waters from above the firmament onto both the earth and the psychic realms. These streams of higher consciousness being poured through the vehicles representing male and female, the conscious and subconscious mind, have a transforming effect on all they touch.

A stream falling onto the earth separates into five parts, and represents the five senses, one of these flowing into the pool as though to form a link between matter and soul. The other vessel pours its stream directly into the pool of inner consciousness.

Violet on the color scale refers to the sign Aquarius and to Truth. The mountain, or goal of attainment, is within view here, but less emphasized than the more immediate quest within the depths. Aquarians make good "fishers for Truth," because they like to delve deep in research to come up with results beneficial to their fellowman.

Another realm of quest is seen here, more distant than the mountain, and that is the stars of heaven. For after the narrow selfish bonds of personal universe of Keys 15 and 16 have been burst asunder, there comes for the first time the awesome glimpse of the magnitude of Creation and the Universe. One realizes the Truth that he and his are not all there is. He sees Man, and the Brotherhood of Man, the ideal of Aquarius. And he sees not just one Sun, but countless Suns— not just one Universe, but myriad universes whirling through space.

The Star: Key 17

Though he glimpses these things now, there is too much to grasp all at once. He is not "there" yet. So he probes the depths of Inner Space in meditation, and at the same time reaches out to study the many religions, the philosophies, the recorded sayings and lives of whatever great Teachers he can contact. The sky is the limit, and he can hardly choose One Way until he has looked at them all. Having been closed for so long, once the door is open and a glimpse of the Light has been seen, he can only be satisfied with the Real thing, and seeks to find it everywhere.

The stars have another meaning. The smaller white ones represent the seven psychic centers of force, each named for a planet. Called *chakras* in Sanskrit, they were known to alchemists as "interior stars."

The Great Central Star is a composite of all the Suns of which one becomes conscious now, and the combined stellar forces which concentrate to bring him upward spiritually.

Comparing this with the Sun in Key 19, you will find it an earlier stage of the same Light, but smaller and less developed. It has the same eight sharp points relating to positive Solar energies, but the eight small points are only budding.

To the Wise Men, thoroughly versed in the heavenly lore, the whereabouts of the Christ child was revealed by a Star. To the man on the spiritual path, the finding of those things represented in this Key will lead him on without fail, to the Christ. But not those who use this knowledge in the employ of Herod, the king of "this world" who seeks to destroy the Christ within lest he lose his throne to this hidden threat.

Wise Men know The Star and follow It alone, because they know where it leads, and they know Who the Real King is!

Jewels of the Wise

AN INKLING OF THE ENSTAR

Out of the dew of the evening
There came a glint of light from afar—
The light from a far-off star.

It uses the dew drop for its prism
To focus its rays on me.
Light had been traveling for centuries
Just to change some atom in me.

So never think any effort too great
If only to bring a smile—
It is always worthwhile.
Perhaps the smile won't be born
Until another morn
When there is no one to see.

Maybe it's just a word of truth that you speak
That will help some over a Mountain peak.
Be it ever so great or ever so small
Remember that words are tall.
They affect one and all.

Heard or unheard to conscious ear,
They take their effect, never fear.
So as we stroll through this life or others,
Let us remember to try to
                              Be Brothers.

Memoirs of a Mystic, by Earl W. Blighton

The Star: Key 17

Path 29
The Corporeal Intelligence

Organization *Sign Pisces*

Key 18

THE MOON

Letter Q   **Qoph – Back of Head**

The Moon has risen from her seat as High Priestess to reign supreme in the heavens, during this fourth stage of spiritual unfoldment. As Priestess in Key 2, she provided the ethereal substance from which all is made, but now works from a higher level to transmute this substance, so that the vehicle of man may become sufficiently spiritualized to receive the Light of Christ. As the Sun is Mediator between God and Nature, the Moon mediates between Sun and Nature.

The focal point of Key 17 The Star was the pool of Aquarius where the Water-Bearer worked to transmute pure waters; now this has become the "Wine of Pisces" (or Yesod, ninth Sephirah of the Moon) and the reduced essential of all things. Here the focus point has lifted, and the pool slips partly below the range of vision. The center of interest is the Path leading up from the home of the Crayfish, a deep freshwater crustacean, to the mountain top.

This indicates that processes of meditation as practiced in Key 17 have revealed the Eternal Way and brought us to the foot of the actual Path we are at last ready to climb. Here is the final journey "home," when man, like the Prodigal Son, "comes to himself' and realizes that the better life is with his Divine Father, back at the spiritual Source from whence he came.

He emerges from the waters here like the purple crayfish, saturated with the violet color which symbolizes Truth. As a creature out of the sea, it represents the first form of spiritually sentient life.

Jewels of the Wise

This follows the pattern originally assumed by physical life as it came forth from the seas to evolve upon dry land. Spiritual life must at this point step gingerly out from the deeps of the subconscious mind, or the instinctual realm which precedes self-control, to unfold in the higher worlds.

Pisces is a fitting zodiacal sign to rule this Key, for it is the water sign representing oceans, and it physically rules the feet which are the real Pathmakers. In the words of the song,

"Lovely appear over the mountain
The feet of them that preach
And bring good news of peace."

The foot is the symbol of the understanding soul, in its direct relationship with earth. The feet of the Great Ones have long traveled and have shown the way for others to follow. This path leads not to a geographical location, but to higher planes of consciousness, to the Beyond which is in reality the Source.

Pisces is the sign opposite Virgo, where the Hermit stood in Key 9 at the other end of this Path, at the mountain's top. The Hermit indicates the heights reached by Mercury or intellect, from which Wisdom holds forth the lantern of Divine Love to show the Way. But now subconscious mind and soul must climb even further out of its own element, over earth, up the mountain, and ultimately higher than intellect could go.

We have arrived at double-nine here in Key 18 and the soul, represented by the crescent moon, has risen to heights beyond those approachable by conscious mind. Here it holds a greater lantern than that lighted by the intellect, for it is directly illumined by reflection of the Sun's rays; and its Light, in turn illuminates the Path which unfolds like a shining ribbon before the Seeker on the Way.

If you bring the ends of this ribbon together and tie a knot, the Path is finished and its cycle ended, with Past being bound to Future in the Eternal Present. The Hebrew letter-word for this Key is *Qoph* and means "back of the head." It was originally shaped like a knot, and is equivalent to our letter Q. It seems curious that we should approach the back of the head before the front, or Face (next Key); but if you wish to approach a brilliantly lighted room, coming in out of the dark, it conditions your vision to first pass through a dimly lit foyer.

At the top of the mountain will be met the full countenance of the Sun, the Head, and the Authority, but here the approach is from the rear, for behind-the-scenes work is being done first—another Piscean function. This is the time when those forces depicted by the Moon perform the necessary operations of the body and blood of man, to ready his vehicle for the coming influx of solar power and the Light of Christ.

The goddess of previous Key 17 The Star seems to have assumed the attitude of our Lady Moon, looking down benignly upon the work she is performing, with kind concern and steadfast attention. The fishhook of Tzaddi did its work and now she augments it with her "lure" of enchantment, and magnetic attraction. As the Moon pulls the tides, she attempts to draw this Fish from its natural habitat into a high place, against its natural disposition to respond to the pull of gravity. In this sign of the Fish ♓ she uses her dominion over the instinctual and intuitive forces to draw forth from the Waters only that which is wholly True in man, as shown by the color violet. This is the Fruit of the Waters whose work began with The High Priestess and ends with the work of the Great Fisherman.

The higher aspects of the subconscious have risen with the Moon to a place above the earth, from which to lift others, beyond their natural level. Her magnetic powers work through close attention to the evolution of Nature and super-Nature, or the enlightenment of mankind.

The towers imply terminal ends, or openings in a wall which separates the mundane from the spiritual, with the veil having been removed. But, as The High Priestess guarded the sacred temple mysteries from the eyes of the profane, the Risen One is still positioned between the neutral, wisdom-gray tower-pillars to make sure that none comes to the Kingdom who is not first refined and found worthy.

This then is the place where bodies are transformed into finer and more sensitive vehicles to make sure they can stand the influx of the Christ Light when it comes so that it will neither harm them nor fail in its purpose. Christ Light has no common meeting ground with gross, unrefined nature and there must be a breakthrough before this can happen. Actual changes must take place in the blood chemistry and certain work done toward refining the centers as well.

Universal forces help make the change into a higher type of organism that would not be possible in Nature's process of evolution. Jesus said, "Flesh and blood cannot inherit the kingdom of God," (1 Corinthians 15:50) and it is true that a spiritual being cannot pass spirituality to his children through family blood lines, but the children of God must be transformed beings of themselves, regardless of earthly parentage.

Only one who has already passed the three previous stages is able to receive this fourth stage of spiritual attainment called Organization. That is to say, the knowledge gained by meditation as shown in the previous Key 17 is now incorporated into the bodily organism and made part of corporeal or physical existence. Thus the function of Key 18 is called Corporeal Intelligence, or body consciousness, and refers to the collective intelligence of all the cells in the body.

One cannot go through illumination until the vehicle has been transformed from its natural state, and the bodily organs must evolve to an extent which permits higher forms of consciousness to manifest through them. Our own desire for spiritual attainment works toward effecting a change, since any need produces some result, even in nature.

"The night brings counsel." In Job 33:15 it was said, "When deep sleep falleth upon men, in slumberings upon the bed, then He openeth the ears of men and sealeth their instruction, that he may withdraw man from his purpose and hide pride from man." It is during sleep that our active mentality is stilled and the subconscious mind is given free rein to mature the thoughts of the day. It is also a time of rest in which to recuperate from strenuous physical activity, in order that the cells may be repaired and strength renewed.

Some of the physical changes necessary to spiritual unfoldment involve changes in blood chemistry and cell structure. These processes are controlled by subconscious activity. The Yods falling from the sky like raindrops are colored red and yellow to indicate that a vital life force is present in the blood along with the elements of its chemical composition. This depicts the descent of life Force by the Will of God into bodily conditions, somewhat as Spirit manifesting.

The phase of the Moon is shown increasing on the positive or "Mercy" side of the Tree of Life. Before complete realization, the Life-Power molds bodies without their conscious knowledge, but later one may consciously share in the Work.

The Work of the Moon is represented as the solar radiance reflecting into the personal sphere of activity. We encounter this reflection before facing the actual radiance itself. The operation of the Moon precedes the experience of the Sun, and thus recedes behind it in time. It represents the state just before perfected control of the ruling authority of the Sun; as the approaching Light shines on ahead by reflection.

The great work of the alchemist is called the work of the Moon and the Sun, aided by Mercury. As you grow in the Work you come to recognize your body and all things as spiritual in their essence. Then does your physical vehicle become a true Temple of God, not made by hands. It is at this point that one is ready to tread the Path in earnest. The feet refer symbolically to the Sephirah Understanding. Here one begins the Return to what he faintly remembers he really is.

The dry land of manifestation emerges from the deeps of Cosmic Mind-Stuff, out of which all form proceeds. This plane of universal subconscious refers to Yesod, or Sphere of the Moon on the Tree of Life. It is more often called the seat of the Vital Soul and automatic consciousness. This represents the completion of involution, preceding the next and final stage of spiritual evolution. The evolving states of consciousness manifest here first as the stone, representing the dense mineral kingdom, then the water-plant, its leaves pointed upward as though aiming high, reminiscent of the meaning of Sagittarius. More cultivated vegetation continues into the field to show Nature's progress.

A primitive form of animal life, the crustacean, is climbing from its habitat in the deep, its shell typifying the earlier stages of unfoldment at which time one still feels separated both from the aspect of Nature and from the realm of Spirit. It represents instinctive energy. The jackal and dog show higher forms of intelligence, both the wild or uncontrolled, and the tamed and controlled form of canine species. Like dogs baying at the moon, they are of the lower state of natural mind or intellect, afraid because the only light they have is a reflected one. They know not what lies in the mysterious area beyond the portals which mark the boundary between the known and the unknown.

The scarab, a beetle sacred to the Egyptians, pushes along its egg, coated with mud, until it hatches from the warmth of the sun. The scarab's egg was considered a symbol of the Sun itself, being carried in silence through the night, or, winter, prior to its resurrection and birth into Light.

The towers form a gateway between the field of well cultivated experience and the limits of ordinary knowledge, acting as boundaries of the great Unknown through which one must tread to reach the Heights. The towers show the last outpost of humanity on the Way. The only light they receive is that of reason, admitted by one small window high up in each tower. So they see little and understand less of the Eternal way.

At this early stage on the Path, the young-in-Truth, represented by the violet sea-creature, is barked at and urged away by the savage warnings of untrained minds, and even by friendly, for-your-own-good interference, as shown by the jackal and dog.

The Moon: Key 18

The undulation of the Path suggests the cyclic nature of all progress, the ups and downs, the high points and the low, but in an ever-rising scale, until it reaches the top of the mountain. One travels more than the actual distance, due to dips in the road. But these are necessary in grading the Path to facilitate travel, rather than going straight up. One must not be dismayed by down cycles; the total progress is upward.

To those seeking a way in the desert, paths made by jackals proved easiest to follow, avoiding as they did the difficult valleys or precipices. Thus was the jackal, reminiscent of Anubis, called "the Opener of Ways." He also guarded the Path so that only those who knew God might pass.

The Moon has sixteen larger and sixteen smaller rays, a total of thirty-two, referring to the thirty-two Paths of Wisdom as the thirty-two modes of human conscious energy are called on the Tree of Life—twice as many as the rays of the Sun on the next Key 19.

These are the thirty-two forces which together weave the vesture of the human body about the personality. The "white work" of the Moon holds the secret of building the mystical temple of regenerated humanity. King Solomon's temple was a Type mystically built to foreshadow this work according to proportions divinely-revealed.

Whereas Kether represents the Vast Countenance, Qoph may be said to represent the Radiant Darkness behind the Countenance which first concentrates in Kether and then emanates forth as the Ten Sephiroth, the effects of its Power. The number associated with Qoph is 100, called the sum of all perfections, or the sum of the Ten Sephiroth multiplied by themselves ($10 \times 10 = 100$). More literally this represents the ten unutterable Sephiroth brought into manifestation through self-contemplation, then multiplied by the manifested Sephiroth of the Tree of Life to total 100, and this is called the "key to the bringing forth of Form."

The Yods

The Yods in Tarot first appear as the blue cap of The Hermit, Key 9. Next, in Key 14 Temperance, we find five yellow yods of flame dropping from the torch of Michael upon the eagle's head, to effect a transformation.

In Key 16 The Tower and Key 18 the yods dripping from heaven are colored like flames, yellow with a smaller red yod at the lower point. There are twenty-two of these in Key 16 to represent the twenty-two Hebrew letters, and they are arranged in geometric patterns.

The eighteen yods in Key 18 encircle the sides and lower portion of the Moon, somewhat reminiscent of the cup of a chalice. In certain other versions this Key shows drops of blood coming down from the Moon.

In The Sun Key 19 are thirteen orange yods from the Sun. Older versions show drops of living gold to indicate supreme spiritual riches raining down upon them.

The Moon: Key 18

Path 30
The Collective Intelligence

Regeneration *Planet The Sun*

Key 19

THE SUN

Letter R **Resh – Countenance**

He has set a tent for the Sun, which comes forth like a bridegroom leaving his chamber, and like a strong man runs its course with joy. Its rising is from the end of the heavens, and its circuit to the end of them, and there is nothing hid from its heat.

The Sun is the Source of practically all the energy we have, its life-giving rays providing all the heat and light, food, fuel, and power which sustain life on this planet, or any other in our system. It even makes the weather, causing winds through warming and cooling of air. The moisture which drops to earth as rain results from drops drawn by the sun up into the clouds.

Very little of the sun's total light and energy ever reaches the earth, and much that is directed our way bounces back from the outer atmospheric shell. But that little we receive is the reason our globe is not pitch dark, is not frozen, dead, nor airless—but has the light, warmth, color and Life given by the Sun. In fact everything we look at is the result in one way or another of solar power.

Its powerful gravitational pull holds the earth on its oval path, and all the other planets in their orbits, as they move round the sun.

Jewels of the Wise

The Sun is the Center and undisputed head of our solar system, the power that holds us all in balance, surpassed only by the greater Head, our God Who created it. Neither the planets nor their moons have any light within themselves. They appear as shining stars in the sky only because they act as mirrored balls which reflect the light of the sun as it strikes their atmosphere.

The Sun is fully illumined throughout, with no dark side, and no dark comers to hide in. More than a lamp set on a hill, it is a ball of blazing Light set in the middle of our solar system, the pivot and hub of it all, the nucleus of the cell.

The Illumined being also becomes a Sun (Son) who shines out from all sides unto those who come nigh, and must not hide his light under a bushel. He differs from the old religionist who knew only reflected planetary light and hearsay truths, who had no experience nor understanding of them. The true Son is Light, and must become ever more aware that he is a source of illumination to those about him. In him must be no darkness at all; as he becomes increasingly aware of the Light, it grows in intensity and measure. The bright face of the Sun searches out any darkness lurking within the seeker approaching him in the Way; the Christ exposes and drives out any darkness as you approach the Light.

When the Light of Christ fully infuses the earth, it will search out all things in every place, and none shall find a hiding place. Whoso tries to flee from it will but run into his own faulty shadow materializing in every place he turns, until it becomes unbearable and he must shed it, with the faults that cause it.

But as he becomes a Son, transparent, he will cast no shadow but both receive light and emit it.

The previous Key 18 The Moon brought us through stages of physical transformation, wherein our lives and bodies were lifted from below and refined. Now in this fifth stage of spiritual unfoldment, the ultimate stage of transformation has been reached, where the Christ Light is absorbed by the prepared being, and man becomes reborn as a little child who knows himself to be in truth a Son of God. Yet he could tell no one how he knows nor how it happened, nor as yet how to use it. Regeneration is the function of this step.

The Light which has been growing and fed both from afar (Key 17 The Star) and from near (Key 18 The Moon) has now come to its own, like the little bear "just right" to perform its life-giving function. It has been lifted up, as our own Lord was lifted up into the heavens, no longer of any "sign" or earthly attribute, but ruler of his own universe.

Christ is the head of the church, said Paul; and the Sun, when realized, becomes the Radiant Head and ruler of our lives. The essence of Christ within our bodily temple becomes the ruler thereof, when we open the door to his knock and bid the Only Begotten of God to come in and sup with us. The Head of anything is that which takes charge and authority. The average man lets his mortal brain or heart do this, from an earthly basis. But the Son means spiritually to man all that the sun means physically to the earth and planets.

Resh, as the Hebrew letter of this Key, looks like an elongated Yod with a line pointed like a ray to send its Life Force down. It corresponds to our letter R, and translated from the Hebrew means "Face, Head, or Countenance." The word "countenance" is also related to the Latin for "contain," and implies that it is within itself.

Collective Intelligence is the name of this Path, for not only does the Sun "contain" but it also collects and distributes the energy and power of Life.

Some of the ancient Mysteries taught that the head was the ruler of the physical body, while the heart was ruler of the spiritual. They really meant the Central Self, rather than the heart. The head is called the shaper of form in the sense that it directs the energies of the individual. A face is shown on the Sun here to bring out the fact that the Solar Being is a great living intelligence.

While the heavenly image of the Complete Being shows only a head or face, the children depict the two halves of man's consciousness, the intellect (boy) and the subconsciousness (girl). Both play an equal part here, and their former positions have been reversed, the girl placed at the right, and the boy at left. This time they are looking at each other with hands (the twin or Gemini part of the body) joined.

The Yod between their heads also indicates a living correlation between the two states of consciousness and shows that they are united in Mind. The six yods on either side remind one of Key 6 The Lovers (Adam and Eve). The yods themselves represent droplets of living gold, radiant energy falling from the Sun to permeate the earth with Life, Light and Love. The Creative Light of this fluidic radiance is employed by God to maintain the Universe and all that is therein.

Orange is used both as a solar color, and to represent Gemini, or Key 6 The Lovers. New mental attitudes and attributes of personality are descending from the Sun. Thirteen is the total number of yods, and is an ancient mystic number representative of the Self within. This results from the combination for the Self whose number was One, plus its composite number twelve for its twelve parts. The same teachings inferred that man's animal soul, his lunar nature, was made up of seven elements, while his body was composed of five elements.

The children represent the early stages of man's spiritual awareness that he has become a new creature and an embodiment of solar consciousness, a begotten Son of God. They have emerged from the depths of experience and stand as new creatures in Christ, fresh as newborn babies with nothing to be ashamed of, therefore nothing to conceal. They have the transparency of the very Wise who only seem complicated to the ignorant who cannot comprehend simplicity. "Why aren't you like me?" ask the foolish, "so that I might understand you?" The Wise man knows better than to explain. They will know when their time comes.

The newborn in Christ have emerged in purity from the compounded misinterpretation of man's teachings, as lotus from the mire. They know because they have experienced the Christ and are no longer dependent on what someone in the past has said or written, yet they now reverence more than ever the words of the Master, feeling their very real kinship with him, even as adopted brothers. They have made the transition coveted by all the sages, from the human state to the Divine.

The sunflowers appear like images of the sun, with double circles and rayed petals. There are supposed to be four full flowers shown, plus a fifth one about to open. These represent the four "kingdoms" over which man has been given dominion, plus the "fifth kingdom" referring to the new regenerated humanity which is just now coming into manifestation. Compare the rays of the flower with another symbol of the Sun, a lion's face surrounded by a mane, his hair standing out as rays.

The Sun itself is shown with eight straight positive rays which are the same as those of the Star in Key 17. But the little nubby points then undeveloped have now grown out to full wavy length. These curved lines or negative rays indicate that the feminine aspect of the Life-Power has developed to become equally as important as the masculine energy of the Sun and no longer subordinate in function, but trained in a better way. Eight is a number symbolic of solar energy.

It is shown yellow, instead of white as with The Fool, because it is intended to depict our actual orb, whereas the White Sun indicated the greater Spiritual Sun behind our own, and around which it revolves. The three straight lines between each ray refer to the activities of integration, balance, and disintegration. Their sum total of forty-eight indicates the twelve-fold nature of the One Power multiplied by the four elements, carried here to its highest degree.

The symbolism of 5 is emphasized further in that there are five rows of stone comprising the wall. In this case, the number refers to experiences drawn through the use of the five senses, which do give actual reports up to a point, though not all the way. Stone indicates whatever solid Truth has been gleaned from their lessons.

The Sun has risen above "the walled Garden of Truth" to manifest its glory unto all who may receive. "I, if I be lifted up, shall draw all men to me." The children gesture with hands to show themselves free from all barriers which might have slowed their spiritual growth. A wall relates this symbol to Cheth of Key 7, the letter relating to speech. The children are not fenced in by speech stemming from sense experience. They have become free of this, and gone beyond, having accepted the Light of a New Way.

The green growth emphasizes work of the sun's vitalizing rays, the physical sun of our solar system in harmony with Nature.

The horse was one of the symbols of solar power, and a former version of the Tarot showed a child riding upon a white horse. The Biblical book of Revelation mentions one seated upon a white horse, who is called Faithful and True.

The double ring in which the children are dancing suggests that in the inner circle they are joined as one, but in the outer work, they may diverge in direction and remain united. The grassy rings appear as a reflection of the Sun and its rays upon the face of Earth. The Center is One, the inner portion correlating with the disk of the Sun itself; the outer portion is as the divergent rays which move straight out in all directions from the center. Yet both are part of One Way.

> *"Let the children come to me, and do not hinder them; for to such belongs the kingdom of God. Truly, I say to you, whoever does not receive the kingdom of heaven like a child shall not enter it."* (Luke 18:16-17)

The Sun: Key 19

Path 31
The Perpetual Intelligence

Realization

Planet Pluto

Key 20

JUDGEMENT

Letter Sh　　　　　　　　　　　　**Shin – Tooth**

For judgement I am come into the world. (John 9:39)
Out of thine own mouth shall I judge thee. (Luke 19:22)

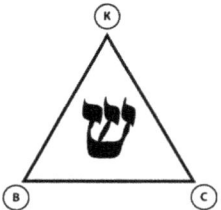

The three flames may be related to the Supernal creative triad on the Tree of Life, *Kether, Chokmah,* and *Binah.* The fool wears over his heart the emblem of the triple Flame, and a symbol of *Shin* is drawn at the lower right of his cloak. In some older versions The Fool is placed here, before Key 21.

Like the Hebrew letter *Shin* itself, man's spiritual nature has a threefold aspect. Three flames are rising from a single base of the letter, as though one large fire was expressing itself in three rays. Similarly, man's own self-consciousness, subconsciousness, and the newborn regenerate being are three parts of one whole, depicted here as human figures which the angel is calling forth from a condition of separation, that they may function as one being in newfound liberation.

In Realization, which is the function of this Key, man moves from the limitations of his old three-dimensional existence with its mortal encasement, comparable to the sleep of death, to be transformed into a new awakened consciousness, where one is functioning on all levels simultaneously, and coming into the recognition of his True Being. They have overcome the dense world by standing at right angles to it.

This call is a spiritual summons from a level above the human, but the answer is from his innermost being, which recognizes its divine Source and joyfully reaches to embrace its Own. Another symphony re-sounds all the words he ever spoke.

Man must become attuned to the harmony of the universe, heard by some as the Grand Aum, or as the music of the spheres, when the inner ear has become finely attuned with rising levels of consciousness. A trumpet sounds the reveille to reawaken him by the power of the Divine Word, but actually the call comes from within himself.

The Sound from the trumpet is shown breaking up into seven tones as it comes forth, referring to the powers of the Seven Elohim expressed in Sound, or the Voice of Fire. Similarly, the light in Key 14 Temperance was shown breaking up into the seven rays of the rainbow. There we also depicted the corresponding sound waves in color. The trumpet is an instrument used to proclaim or publish abroad, as with announcing a coming event.

"I heard behind me a loud voice like a trumpet..." (Revelation 1:10), and
"His voice was like the sound of many waters..." (Revelation 1:15)

The Archangel of Water shown here is Gabriel, and being also Archangel of the Moon, he is the invisible power behind The High Priestess Key 2, and director of her subconscious activities. Gabriel means "Strength of God" or "Might of God," and he has come to announce the completion of the Great Work.

It was he who announced to Mary and to Elizabeth the coming birth of a son, each of them a departure from the laws of Nature. He said then, "I am Gabriel who stands in the Presence of God, and

I was sent to speak to you, and to bring you the good news." (Luke 1:19)

The waters of consciousness from The High Priestess have flowed silently and sometimes secretly throughout all of the rest and now come to the reservoir of Binah, the Great Sea of Divine Understanding. Parts of the stream have solidified into icebergs shown in the background. In alchemy this is called the "fixation of the volatile," or arresting of the stream of Consciousness. Judgement also terminates reasoning, the conclusion of which comes about with true Knowing.

In the time of Noah came the first destruction of the world by water, symbolizing the collective subconscious mind, and its flooding over the set boundaries. God promised then that it would never happen thus again, but next time by fire. This is not an earthly fire from below, not even one of human passions, but a spiritual fire descending from God, an invisible purging agent.

John baptized with water for repentance, but said that Jesus "will baptize with the Holy Spirit and with Fire." (Matthew 3:11)

Fire is a symbol of Spirit. It is as mysterious and unknowable as the Spirit itself in essence. Of what is it made and whence does it come? Fire and Spirit are both related to the Divine Life-Breath, and here the tiny spark of divinity in man unites with the Whole Being.

The dictionary defines fire as "the invisible active phase of combustion, manifested in light and heat." Esoterically, Fire is the great crucible in whose nature all things are purged of their impurities, in order to return them again to a simple and pristine state. The dross of sham drops from all it embraces, and the essence of the thing becomes revealed.

God has sometimes appeared in Fire, encompassed with Fire, or has dropped fire from heaven. Deuteronomy 4:24 states, "The Lord thy God is a consuming Fire."

The Fire signs of the zodiac are Aries, Leo and Sagittarius. The planets associated with this Key are Vulcan, the smithy and god of Fire; and Pluto, ruling the fires of Hades.

We not only "die daily" with Paul, but daily rise, resurrected from earth's limitations. The coffins symbolize these restrictions which hold us apart and ignorant of the Real. The figures representing the conscious and subconscious minds have been joined by their offspring and combined essence, the new regenerated being in Light who stands in the middle in the square coffin. He is the true Stone of the wise, rising up out of the restricting encasement.

These coffins have kept apart, without communication, the three separate aspects of the consciousness of one single being. But at the trumpet call, they spring up to this new dimension wherein they are cognizant of each other, and able to work together. This new state is called the Fourth Dimension, and is symbolized by the posture of the figures, standing at right angles to their former horizontal positions. About to step up into the New Heaven and New Earth, this shows them leaving the old heaven and inert earth.

The figures are reversed from their usual positions, for here the man is standing in a passive attitude of adoration, while the woman is actively reaching out, and the child is facing inward, toward the Way from whence he came, now seeking inner guidance. The gray flesh shows that they have overcome all polar opposites, and have blended all duality in wisdom. The position of their arms spells LUX, or the Latin word for Light, sometimes used as a signature among Brothers. Their attitudes on the physical plane have reversed as are all things on the astral, where they are beginning to function.

The Path of this Key is called The Perpetual Intelligence, which recognizes life as eternal, extended into the higher consciousness of Immortality. The new state, represented by the child, is no longer separate but a composite of both.

Water washes the surface of things, or flushes them out, but it cannot dissolve or remove the denser and more crystallized impurities. So at this, the sixth stage of spiritual unfoldment called Realization, the solar Light burns out all that is not of itself. The inner spiritual

Judgement: Key 20

Light cannot be destroyed by spiritual Fire from without, but only increased thereby.

Realization brings a new dimension in consciousness, as the human or personal consciousness approaches the stage of blending with universal consciousness, thus liberating the spiritual body from the material.

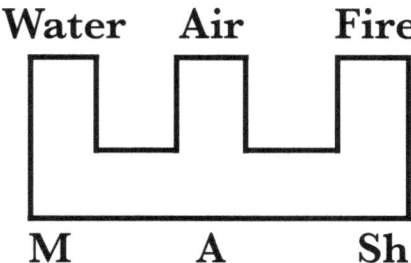

This figure depicts the "universal energy in triple potency of expression." *Shin* is the third Mother letter of the Hebrew alphabet and represents the element of Fire. *Aleph* being that of Air, and *Mem* of Water. These three combine through the Breath of *Aleph* to bring about the completed stage called Earth in the next and last Key. *Shin* as a Hebrew letter is "sh," but as a noun it means "tooth," or "fang." We might call it the Tooth of Fire, or the Fang of Flame, that which breaks down material forms and releases the elements back into the bosom of Nature. "Sh" sounds like an admonition to be silent, and so it is, for idle talk dissipates the potency of the greater spiritual experience.

Just as the Tooth of Judgement breaks down and feeds upon all that is superfluous to our newfound spiritual life, so do the teeth of living beings break down food into component parts in order that these may be correctly digested and channeled for assimilation. When the great Judgement Day arrives for each man, not necessarily with bodily death, his former ideas of separation are broken down. When the Holy Spirit consumes all barriers from his life, the higher consciousness consumes the lower.

Shin was also called the Holy Letter, relating to the fiery Life Breath of the Elohim. It is this letter which is placed at the center of the Divine Name, JHVH or Yahweh in order to form the name "Jesus," as spelled in Hebrew J-H-Sh-V-H, as in Joshua.

Three times has the angel appeared—Raphael in Key 6 The Lovers, where Adam was tested. In Key 14 Temperance Michael appeared, and a new test was applied—that man should prove how far he had come, and whether he was qualified to enter a spiritual path. In Key 20 the end of this spiritual path has been nearly reached. He has already realized the Christ, and now must show his readiness to "rise on the planes."

The angel has come to render decision. Whereas spasmodic flashes of Spirit showed in Key 16 The Tower, Key 20 now brings a continuous recognition of Spirit, not lapsing even in sleep, serving God night and day. This again explains the name of the Path, Perpetual Intelligence.

Justice in Key 11 measures the deeds of everyone and the earthly Karma they have earned; but Judgement measures the soul of man and weights his spiritual merit. No scales are required to weigh and balance this, for Spirit sees the whole Truth instantaneously and knows all that is.

Number symbology in this Key brings out the proportion of five times five, or the square of 5, as used in the banner. This has been called the Magic Square of Mars, in reference to the fifth Sephirah and its fiery quality. It has been noted that this square appears as a window set on high in the heavens through which we may observe from a higher level of understanding. Another interesting reference to number is in the numerical value of the letter *Shin*, which is 300. One hundred or 10 x 10 represents perfection, as the reaching of perfection with *Qoph*; the value of *Resh* is 200, or twice-perfect; *Shin* represents triple perfection, in a summing-up of its three-fold nature in the number 300. (In *Tav*, Key 21, we will have manifested perfection, for the final number 400 will have been brought forth and made solid.)

Judgement: Key 20

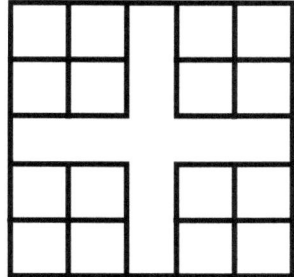

The clouds surrounding the angel form a circle within which the upper and lower halves resemble a number 8, eternity as the circle, and infinity or dominion as 8. The clouds remind one that the substance of those things which appear are of the same stuff as The High Priestess' garment, a form of the element water, and that this tends to veil the light of the Self. However, the twelve rays of light piercing the veil come from the Self. This is the Fire of Chokmah hidden in the depths of the waters of Binah.

Path 32
The Administrative Intelligence
Cosmic Consciousness   *Planet Saturn*

Key 21

THE WORLD

Letter Th   **Tav – Mark**

As long as I am in the world,
I am the Light of the world.

Judgement broke down all barriers in readiness to start over. "And there shall be (and now is) a New Heaven and a New Earth." It is this new state of consciousness that is depicted in Key 21—that of one who has overcome all, and has attained inner and outer perfection. This is the goal of all previous endeavors, and the accomplishment of the Great Work of alchemy.

The Greek word for "world" is *cosmos*, which better describes the meaning of this Key as comprehending the whole universe.

The three figures shown in Key 20 Judgement have merged now into the whole perfect being, perfect because it has risen to become one with the Cosmic Reality. The separate components of personal consciousness, the subconscious, and the newborn spiritual consciousness reached their highest state in Key 20, and have now merged into One, the integrated consciousness of Realization. No longer are these areas of awareness separated into assorted closed pockets to be used one at a time, but have come all together in one piece to permit simultaneous functioning on all counts.

That this is a living state is shown by the green wreath of Nature surrounding the central figure. The growth and power of the living

Word is evident, for it is composed of twenty-two leaves, symbolizing the twenty-two letters of the Hebrew alphabet, which construct speech. Each leaf is of triple-formation, to denote the three stages in any process of vital growth—those of coming into effect, or integration; balance, or equilibration; and thirdly, disintegration.

The wreath is called the Crown of the Initiate, "given only unto him who masters the four guardians," and enters into the presence of the whole Truth. It is the wreath of victory woven to form the Crown of overcoming.

This is tied with red ribbon in the form of two figure-eights, the number of dominion and infinity. Their red color shows the field of activity as being in the physical realm. The only part which shows is a segment shaped like X, this being one form of the cross, itself an ancient method of writing the Hebrew letter *Tav*, or T, and is used as a signature by some.

Here the ties form the signature or witness of completion of the work of the living Word, as they bind all its component parts into a perfected whole, and form a framework within which the realized Self may function.

The zero-formation of the wreath carries us through to the next state of The Fool, as though a circle had been completed, twenty-two Keys having opened a great Door into the Mysteries of the Ages. Where once The Fool blew forth his Breath of Divine Life by means of the Word, he now prepares to gather the fruit of that resounding Word, in the dense field of the world. But as with all circles of evolution, the motion is spiral; the end of the circle is higher than the beginning, and is no end at all, because its upward movement is infinite.

The Fool stood looking outward and upward to that which must be accomplished, but The World is looking within to the Self where the kingdom of heaven has been discovered. Together 0 and 21 show the beginning and the end.

Into the hands of this Self-controlled being are all powers given of dominion and authority, and of the uses of all positive and negative forces of Nature. He grasps the twin spheres of electricity which whirl in two opposite directions to denote the dual nature of Universal Force, positive and negative, as well as involution and evolution. A glowing ellipse of white light surrounds them.

The figure itself is neither male nor female, but a perfectly balanced being or androgyne. This fact is veiled by a violet scarf shaped like the letter *Kaph* of Key 10. An ancient Hebrew word is *dahm*, which meant both "world" and "that which is hidden or veiled." The posture of this figure is akin to the alchemical symbol for Sulphur, or that Divine Fire which is the heart of the great Mystery.

The violet, or Truth-color of the scarf, shaped like the letter *Kaph* (which means "grasp" or "closed hand") denotes that here the grasp of Truth itself has become complete. "The Truth shall make you free." It is as though the only support to be considered here is the Hand of God bearing one up. The red wreath upon the head of the individual is the fruition of the green wreath worn by The Empress, which developed flowers in Strength, and now is a full-grown and activated crown of Nature.

This thirty-second Path of Wisdom is called Administrative Intelligence, for he who possesses it is brought into a condition of responsibility for cooperating with the Creator of all, and to do his part in helping to direct the administration of the universe. This Path is said to "direct all the operations of the seven planets and concur therein."

Because he has left behind the error-driven consciousness of old and has entered into the stream of divine consciousness, he becomes totally cooperative with the Will of God. For it is not that he has gained powers, so much as that he has opened himself up to the Divine Conscious Energy of the Creative Expression of all things—in other words to God. The state of Being represented here is that of functioning fully with Self. The personal consciousness which found termination in *Shin* is now superseded by the higher realization, or Cosmic Consciousness.

"The true light that lightens every man was coming into the world. He was in the world, and the world was made through him, yet the world knew him not." (John 1: 9) The old world of matter yields its control as the new spiritual world enters to take it over. "In an instant," said a Sufi named Shabistari, "rise from time and space. Set the world aside and become a world within yourself." Like a new orb launched into space, *Tav* has Become.

Until now he has been in the process of preparing himself for this mission, of working through discipline toward perfection. The Celestial Dancer did not achieve perfect command over his vehicle and over the forces of gravity without extensive practice and rigid discipline. It takes years to train a prima ballerina, one who seems to defy gravity in graceful leaps and whirls; and the same holds true for the spiritual Dancer, who dwells upon earth and uses it, but is never held nor bound by it. He is set free from its former limitations, not by being excused from or escaping them, but by facing and overcoming them. Then he is ready to inherit the Crown of the Kingdom given to one who overcomes. Here he touches from within the Crown of Kether at the top of the Tree of Life.

The planet Saturn is assigned to this Key, he being considered the stern teacher and disciplinarian who seems to restrict one's free will to do as he pleases. Actually it is only through this discipline that one is enabled to become the Dancer. Saturn makes you "toe the mark" until you know it so well that it becomes a habit to discipline yourself, and outside restrictions are no longer needed when Self-discipline has become an integral part of your being; and only then can you know true freedom, for you now have command of the very things which obstructed you before.

The element Earth is also represented by *Tav*. Saturn is a planet of earth-nature, and here that element reaches its ultimate. For the squeeze of external pressures have produced the hardest substance, that perfect diamond at the core of all the Radiant One flashing its

The World: Key 21

Light, clear and most durable. It is in earth, rather than in abstraction, that one finds the fullest opportunity to serve.

In mythology Saturn swallowed his own children, and on the Path of *Tav* all previous modes of consciousness are swallowed up. (Thus it logically follows *Shin*, the Tooth.) The Hebrew name for Saturn, seventh planet of the ancients, was *Shabbathai*, from whence we derive "sabbath," the day of cessation from labor, because the world has been made, and Work finished. Twenty-one is three times seven, and thus a spiritual manifestation of the law of seven. Saturn also has to do with Time, otherwise called a crystallization of Eternity.

The four creatures shown at the corners of the Key represent the four elements of earth as depicted by the fixed signs of the zodiac, sometimes called the four directions of Space. In Key 10 The Wheel of Fortune these same figures show the bull turned inward away from the world of material form, toward the field of abstract Energy; but here he has turned about to break the pattern of involution, and to move outward to work in the world of form.

The man represents the fixed-Air sign, Aquarius; the lion, fixed-Fire sign Leo; the eagle, fixed-Water sign Scorpio; and the bull, fixed-Earth sign Taurus. Each element is presented in its most stable condition, called "fixed" or solid, and this denotes the materialization or crystallization of form, which Saturn influences. Yet within the seeming bounds of the elements and the weight of matter, the Self soars free.

Twenty-one is the completion of that which was promised or foreshadowed in Key 12 Suspended Man, where was shown the upside-down reflection of the ultimate Reality, though that was its first outward manifestation. At that point man had suspended himself by a spiritual cord to the goal, which then appeared as the hard gallows shaped like a letter *Tav*. It was the beginning of disciplines. But the goal is now mastered, and the support no longer needed: now he is Self-suspended. Job said, "God hangs the earth upon nothing." When the adult age of twenty-one is reached, spiritually as well as legally, the Dance of Life begins, supported by nothing but Self in perfect equilibrium. Now one begins to express and demonstrate in practice what he has gained or learned in theory and, in taking on complete responsibility, he is released like the baby bird to fly.

And so *Tav* seals his witness of the culmination of the Work leading to Realization and Cosmic Consciousness. He makes his cross or mark, *"Tav"* his signature. Jesus, too, culminated his earthly work with a cross which has become his symbol and signature in the Christian world. Yet the word *Tav* itself is spelled with two Hebrew letters—*Tav* and *Vav*—signifying completion and continuation.

"I am the Alpha and the Omega, the beginning and the ending." (Revelation 22:13). This is the Ascension.

The World: Key 21

Jewels of the Wise

www.ingramcontent.com/pod-product-compliance
Lightning Source LLC
Chambersburg PA
CBHW041138110526
44590CB00027B/4061